THE ECONOMICS OF
MANAGERIAL DECISION

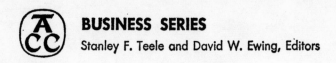

BUSINESS SERIES

Stanley F. Teele and David W. Ewing, Editors

CHESTER R. WASSON
California Western University

THE ECONOMICS OF MANAGERIAL DECISION:
Profit Opportunity Analysis

New York

APPLETON-CENTURY-CROFTS

Division of Meredith Publishing Company

To the memory of

ROBERT W. MURCHIE

who taught me more
than I realized at the time

Foreword

To THE BUSINESSMAN, the kind of "economics" that is most important is not the "economics" of the professional economist. The economics of managerial decision begins with different assumptions, proceeds along different lines, and ends with different concepts and conclusions than does the economics of aggregate analysis. The former is what Chester Wasson deals with in this book. He looks at profits, decision making, forecasting, competition, pricing, costs, and related issues—the same topics covered in conventional economics texts, but from the unique, strategic viewpoint of the corporate manager, rather than from that of the professional economist.

Understanding and applying managerial economics is a highly creative task. It is the key to much of the industrial progress that people in business, government, and labor hope this country will achieve in the next generation. Courses in this area are among the most important ones taught in business schools. In addition, probably no aspect of management training, whether it be formally conducted in university programs or informally carried out under the home reading lamp at night, is more readily learned than managerial economics.

This volume is one of the first of a series of original paperback texts by eminent authorities on business administration, designed for use in business school courses and in-company training programs. Instructors can use it either as a basic text or as a supplementary text, viz., part of the package of teaching materials used in their courses. The author has sought to distill a large mass of material into the comparatively brief space of this book. It represents a compact analysis of highlights and key topics only. Hence businessmen, too, should find it useful in enlarging their understanding of management problems.

Stanley F. Teele
David W. Ewing

Preface

THIS BOOK WAS put together to meet a need I felt, and which seems to be shared by others, for an up-to-date discussion of those economic concepts that offer the greatest help in estimating the profit opportunities implicit in business decision alternatives, whether the problem be a classroom case or one played for keeps at the plant.

Except for Joel Dean's pioneering work, most books on managerial economics seem to ignore the problem of product competition which stands at the top of the everyday agenda in nearly every business. (In a recent survey of large businesses, all respondents listed product as one of their top policy problems, only 3 out of 5 listed price.) Edward Chamberlain might as well have been a voice crying out in the emptiness of Death Valley for the last thirty years for all of the attention that has been paid to the full implications for business decision of his concept of product differentiation. Part of this neglect may be due to the extreme focus on the macro side which has dominated economic thought for the past generation, and for the accompanying desire for precise mathematical formulations. As J. M. Clark points out in his recent lucid exposition of *Competition as a Dynamic Process,* the desire for precisionism cannot afford to take cognizance of the phenomenon of product competition and the psychological concept of product this imposes. The result has been a sterile emphasis on those concepts of economics lending themselves theoretically to precision treatment, and a total disregard of data availability which students with business experience recognize and shun.

The extreme mathematical approach of some of these works also neglects the real need to inculcate a balanced analytical use of the kinds of quantitative material really available, an approach that puts continued stress on the absolute necessity for the use of available quantitative estimates while critically examining their value and fully appreciating the degree of approximation involved in the use of the most precise information in forecasting decision outcomes.

Accordingly, this work couples a discussion of the uses of the simpler analytical tools—which form the mainstay of every experienced analyst—with a discussion of the economic concepts best adapted to estimating profit possibilities in a dynamic business situation in which innovation is the only source of true profit. When using the book in connection with classroom cases, the instructor should stress the need to be specifically quantitative about every decision. Simultaneous emphasis must be directed to the lack of precision in many of the quantities used and the need to examine critically their meaning for the given decision.

To this has been added some discussion aimed at an understanding of the capabilities of the more common special mathematical techniques—largely but not exclusively for computer use —with which the business manager must increasingly work and which he must really understand in order to wisely use the data resulting from their use.

One very important intellectual debt must be acknowledged. My former officemate at Case Institute of Technology, Prof. Samuel J. Mantel, Jr., first stimulated my interest in the subject of managerial economics, and I learned much from his discussions with students both inside his classroom, and in the office. Many aspects of this discussion owe their origin to his presentations, but three must be acknowledged specifically: 1) the concept of *engineering to cost*, treated under the chapter on price, 2) the discussion of working capital in the chapter on investment, and 3) the discussion of the use of frequency distribution analysis.

C.R.W.

Contents

Foreword   vii

Preface   ix

1. Economic Concepts Needed for the Analysis of Business
   Figures   1

2. Pinpointing the "How Much" of a Decision   22

3. Understanding and Forecasting the Demand and Supply
   Situation   55

4. Competition: Management of the Product Variable   77

5. Price: The Tactical Weapon of Competition   112

6. Determination of Economic Cost   147

7. Planning for Capital Investment   163

8. Tools Useful for Comparing Alternatives   181

Selected Bibliography   219

Index   223

1

Economic Concepts Needed for the Analysis of Business Figures

THE CONCEPT OF profit is not entirely like the weather—a lot of people do try to do something about it. But their forecasts are less dependable than the weatherman's, and their appraisals of how much has been achieved are about as trustworthy as the reports on the size of the hailstones in that sudden squall. Like the weather, however, the only really important aspect of profit is the forecast of the opportunity for it. It is the forecast that determines plans.

Forecasting of any sort requires the analysis of the meaning for the future of some kind of information—usually quantitative—about the near and distant past. Since only very specific forecasts are of much planning value, the forecaster must use some concepts of the relationship between this past and the present and future time as a framework to give his figures meaning for the decisions he must make. The choice of the proper framework (or model) is crucial. No matter how accurate the figures or how skillful their manipulation, the wrong model will usually lead to the wrong answer. The tools for their manipulation are also important, of course, in squeezing out hidden meaning, but only within the chosen framework.

For business decision, the framework which imparts really useful meaning consists of a handful of economic concepts and

1

models. The basic concept is the view of competition as *product differentiation*, first developed by Chamberlain in his historic work on monopolistic competition. The conceptual yardsticks by which we must fit our figures into this model are those of *alternate opportunity*, the *uncertainty discount*, and the *time discount*.

The Basic Model: Monopolistic Competition

Business decision is competitive decision and must be based on the right conceptual model of the mechanics of successful competition. That model is monopolistic competition [1] (including what some economists differentiate as "differentiated oligopoly"), a model which focusses on product as the major decision variable, with product understood in its widest psychological meaning, as all elements contributing to consumer value.

This model starts from five basic postulates:

1. Product is a bundle of services, not a homogeneous physical entity, and the desire for the same service may, in fact, be satisfied by different kinds of physical products. Each service has a different value for each potential customer. Some values may be inherent in the physical product, but others may be associated with it through the terms and manner of sale, derived from the culture in which the product is produced, or induced by outside forces, including the various forms of sales promotion.

2. Successful bundles contain specific differential elements with a special attraction for some specific large core segment of the market. With respect to this core segment, the seller has a monopoly of greater or lesser value. But for other potential customers,

---

[1] Those interested in the game of finespun scholastic speculations separate the "differentiated oligopoly" situation in which the "competitors" are a finite few from "monopolistic competition" situations in which the number of "competitors" is large. From a theoretical point of view, this distinction ignores or downgrades the central condition of product differentiation, since it rests on a physical-product-centered definition of competition. This is not compatible with the concept of product as a differentiated bundle of services central to monopolistic competition theory. In practice, it has no significance either, since few industries fit either pattern completely, and the aim of the manager must be the same in either case: to locate or develop a specialized market segment in whose service he can excel.

these particular differentiating elements have no significant value, or may even have negative value. In relation to this fringe group, the seller is in competition with others offering the same product services the fringe customers do value in his offering. This means he may be in competition with different sellers for different fringe segments, and with different physical product forms in many cases.

3. Since the customer's demand valuation is the algebraic sum of his psychological evaluation of each of the product characteristics, product content is an intertwined variable with price in competitive management decision.

4. The primary aim of the seller is to so combine the twin variables of product and price as to gain a substantial differential advantage over competition with some important segment of the market.

5. Management acts in the knowledge that its actions do influence the decisions and actions of the closer competitors. Product characteristics, in the broad sense in which product is defined here, are more difficult to copy than is price structure. The seller can construct a product bundle for which his special abilities are better adapted than those of close competitors. Thus, both in practice and in theory, emphasis tends to be on the product side of strategy.

What one man can do, another can find a way to copy, sooner or later. Thus all differential advantages are temporary, and the successful can remain so only through continual innovation. This product-centered model of competition thus focusses on the role of innovation, in both physical product and its marketing aspects, as the primary source of business profit. Because of the transitory nature of innovation, the market is in a constant state of flux. Feedback of the results of any decision resulting from constant innovation rules out any tendency to stable equilibrium.

The central position of innovation rules out, in turn, any possibility of definitive solutions in marketing decisions. Innovation cannot be programmed on a computer. There can be no cookbook recipes for successful decision, and the best of theory can only hope to help us arrive at a rough approximation of the probabilities for success of imaginative enterprise. This does not imply that the theory is not useful but argues instead for using as much help as can be had from careful attention to it.

In this respect, the business manager is only in a somewhat more difficult position than the engineer when the latter must rely on the basic theories of physics, chemistry, and the other more stable sciences to develop new design. Designs do not come out of indexed files. The safety factor principle of all engineering is simple recognition of the approximation always present when applying even the best-researched scientific models to practical design decision. But the theories do tell the engineer both what to measure and how to measure it, and thus reduce the element of uncertainty to a livable level. Theory furnishes the basic analytical concepts that go into the model and the yardsticks for getting the figures that fit these concepts.

The Basic Economic Value Concepts

The concepts into which the figures used for profit forecasting must be fitted are: demand and supply, production, competition, cost, price, and capital investment. All six of these concepts have a meaning in common usage which, for the purposes of analysis, must be restricted in some ways, broadened in others.

DEMAND AND SUPPLY

Economic demand is not simple want or desire and *is only indirectly for some objective product or service.* It is the willingness and ability of a prospective purchaser to sacrifice something of value—ultimately, money—for some service, or more usually a group of services, offered by some seller. This service may, it is true, be embodied in a physical object which is the subject of the actual purchase. But even in this case, the actual physical characteristics of the item bought may simply serve as a physical symbol which convinces the buyer he has acquired the psychological service desired. The object itself may have no inherent ability to render the actual satisfaction. The girl who buys Arpege perfume may be seeking glamor, not just a nice odor, which is all the perfume imparts. Her father may proudly park a Cadillac convertible on the drive because it symbolizes status, not just well-built transportation. But his neighbor may buy the same make because he likes well-built mechanical contrivances to play around with. The satisfactions furnished by the physical product may be quite different for different customers.

The potential demand we wish to forecast, then, is not either a quantity or schedule of quantities of some specific physical object, but quantities of unsatisfied desires of varying intensities. Each prospective customer has placed on each service some value with which he is willing to part for the satisfaction of the particular bundle of desires he is interested in, or more usually, there is some value with which he will part if his interest in the satisfaction combination is properly stimulated by dramatization of the benefits that would appeal to him.

This demand is a variable, not a fixed figure, because different individuals value different characteristics differently, and the marginal value of the money given up differs between individuals, e.g., between the oil millionaire and the day laborer. The quantity sold—the effective demand—will depend on price, on availability in the trade (distribution), on the knowledge of the product and its benefits brought about by advertising and personal selling, on the expectation of price trends, on the state of taste at the moment, and many other factors. In economic texts, the principal attention is usually focussed on the price variable, and demand is traditionally depicted as a curve or line sloping downward to the right (price depicted in vertical measure, quantity in the horizontal), or occasionally as a table. In real life, this price-quantity relationship, after other important factors are held more constant than they usually are, may approach the smooth continuity of the textbook curve. More usually, it obviously does not, and no simple equation is likely to state the relationship correctly, if we could measure the factors precisely, which we cannot.

Regardless of our ability to measure the relationship, however, demand is variable at any one point in time, and management decision on price or any of the other sources of variability will influence the amount to be sold, if the enterprise's output and other resources are significant enough to put a dent in the market.

Supply is simply the other side of the demand coin, and just as much a variable. In many ways, in fact, it is more subject to direct management action than is demand, since management has more latitude in its decision as to what it will pay. Those decisions on the offering price for labor, materials, and other resources needed in production and the efforts put forth in making its wants known and in dramatizing them can greatly affect the quantity available, even in the short run.

PRODUCTION

The economic definition of production follows from the definition of demand. Production is the making available of some service for which the customer will pay some price. Production is the creation of potential value.

Value may be created by transforming the physical form of raw materials, e.g., by the refining of ores into metal and the shaping of metal into automobiles. Or it may be created by moving the objects or services to where they are more accessible to the customer (place utility), at the time he most desires them (time utility). The creation of a strong dealer-service network is one of the values for which General Motors is paid when you buy a Chevrolet. Or the value may have been created by an association of the actual product with some otherwise irrelevant satisfaction the customer desires, e.g., cigarettes with the image of virility. As transportation in modern city traffic, the Cadillac has demonstrable deficiencies in comparison with some other makes. But its association with social status is so firmly established that women will wrestle them into crowded parking spots a few blocks from home on weekly shopping trips.

COMPETITION

Since what the customer buys is some kind of satisfaction mix, and the mix bought, even in the same physical product, differs for different customers, your real competitor may furnish a seemingly different product, and someone producing a very similar physical product may not be competing with you at all. Some of Maytag's washing machine competition is the local centralized cleaning and laundering plant, another the local Laundromat, and another, the producer of paper napkins. On the other hand, both the Austin Sprite and the Cadillac Coupe de Ville are undeniably automobiles, but few if any customers are likely to consider them as alternate sources for the satisfactions they seek in an automobile.

Competition is thus a very complex phenomenon, and practically never the simple head-on sort of thing denoted by the athletic frame of reference the term suggests. The marketplace has little resemblance to the World Series or a football stadium. To use mathematical parlance, business is not a zero-sum game.

COST

Economic cost is not a sum of figures in an account book and is usually either more or less than this. Economic cost is alternate opportunity cost. It is the difference in sacrifice between what is done and the next best choice and can be estimated only by means of accurate evaluation of alternate opportunities, including the opportunity to do nothing.

PRICE

The practical economic definition of price has much in common with the broad popular connotation—that which a man is willing to give up in return for some satisfaction. From a decision point of view, this makes price a complex phenomenon rather than a simple one-dimensional one. From what has already been said, it should also be obvious that price means nothing except in terms of a very precise definition of product, in relation to a given potential buyer and the satisfactions he is interested in.

Thus there is no such thing as "pricing above the market" or "below the market" as these terms are loosely used in some of the business literature. Instead, a seller delivers a premium product, or gets some other quid pro quo in addition to the money the objective physical product might otherwise have brought, e.g., a favored position on some future market. And when a buyer pays a premium price, it is not necessarily for the current satisfactions physically built into the objective product, but for some other associations (as in a premium brand perfume) or for some sale-related benefits such as the seller's technical service in the case of an industrial supply line.

CAPITAL INVESTMENT

A capital investment is the purchase of a series of future income flows. Its value is therefore the *discounted probable value* of the best estimate of those income flows, neither more nor less.

The income expected may flow from the capacity of a physical plant and equipment to build some kind of saleable product, or the capacity of a piece of real estate to save rental costs. Or it may flow from a favored position on the market, resulting in a series of sales not otherwise made, because of the purchase of the goodwill of a subsidiary. It may result from the development of a market preference by means of a well-planned sales promotion campaign.

Since the income flows are deferred, their value is in part uncertain, and the extent of this uncertainty must be reflected by reducing the total value to be expected by the percentage of uncertainty. Since the expected value is in the future, this value must in turn be discounted at whatever rate of return is appropriate in view of the firm's alternative uses for the money involved in the meantime.

Since capital investment and all of the other five concepts revolve around some aspect of value, we need some yardstick for value. That yardstick is the value of the best known alternative opportunity.

The One Basic Yardstick: Alternate Opportunity

Value is by its very nature a relative term, i.e., it is measured by comparison with something else. For economic value, that something else is the next best alternative opportunity for cost, profit, product, or whatever item is being evaluated. And for decision purposes, it is a forward-looking term, i.e., it is measured in relation to future opportunities, not past events. It is the difference between the cost which would have been incurred or the profit received and that which would have been there under an alternate course of action or inaction.

Thus the balance sheet does not reveal the profit really resulting to the firm from some given decision. This profit can be determined only on the basis of a calculation showing the difference added to profit by undertaking the action decided upon, as against the *probability result* if that action had *not* been taken. Plus figures can conceal a true loss if the profit proves to be less than might have been realized under a different course of action which was known and available at the time the decision was made. Conversely, what appears on the balance sheet as a loss can disguise a true profit if the loss realized is less than the probable loss in the best available alternative.

Similarly, *economic cost* may be quite a different figure than that appearing on the company books. For example, the cost of production for an additional item is the difference in cost between total production cost for the run including that item and the total cost if production stopped just short of it.

To the buyer, the alternate cost, from some other source, of those portions of the service package he values, determines who the seller's competition is.

The principle of alternative opportunity is more widely discussed in economics under the headings of *incrementalism, marginalism* and *equimarginalism.* These are measured in terms of *discounted value,* and what must be included is determined by the *time perspective.*

Incrementalism is normally used in reference to cost and revenue estimates. Incremental cost is that *change* in cost which would be or is incurred as the result of a decision to *change* the output level, the method of production, the source or quantity of purchase, or any other element affecting cost. In like manner, incremental revenue is that change in revenue resulting from a decision to change any element affecting revenue, e.g., price, promotional methods and intensities, product, distribution methods, order policy, etc. Incremental costs or revenues are thus the difference between total costs or revenues expected under the present situation and those under one proposed alternative.

Marginalism, as used in economics, is both a more refined and a more restricted term, and not as well suited to the needs of management decision as is incrementalism. As generally understood by economists, marginal costs and marginal revenues refer to unit-by-unit changes in output, with examination of costs or revenues at each unit point of change. By inference, this is a narrower concept than that of increments. The latter may compare, for example, the same level of output under alternative systems of production and sale, whereas the margin can only refer to changes within a given system. Both, however, are simply different aspects of alternate opportunity analysis.

Equimarginalism is sometimes used to pinpoint the optimum allocation of resources. The concept means that the last unit of resource input (usually considered as the last dollar's worth added) in each use should yield the same added profit. To put it more concretely, the last dollar added to the advertising appropriation would return the same profit as the last dollar of salary and expense incurred in research and development, likewise in plant and equipment expenditures, or in production wages and salaries, and so on. In every case, the expected return must be discounted both for the uncertainty involved and the delay in revenue.

Application of this principle assumes the presence of some form of diminishing return, and no practical limitation on the use of any resource for a given purpose, short of the point of equality. In practice, studies have shown that some kinds of marginal costs are constant within the range of experience of many kinds of firms. But if resources are really large, this cannot be true for all costs of a given firm at any one time, particularly the important marketing costs. There must always be some practical limit on the amount of profit to be had from increasing advertising expenditures or other sales costs, for example.

An important corollary of the equimarginal principle is that if no equimarginal point can be found—if profits from one use of capital always exceed those from some other necessary use, properly measured—then either the calculation is faulty, or the firm is in a position to farm out the low yield part of the activity to someone else. In fact, this is a frequent practice in industry. Some firms are so much more efficient at marketing than at production, they contract out much of the production. Others excel at production planning and prefer to delegate selling. Some firms have better alternative uses for their investment capital than suppliers, and may buy rather than make something at which they are at least as efficient at producing as the potential supplier. Thus one of the alternatives to be considered in allocating resources is a zero allocation to low yield activities.

The equimarginal principle can never be exactly applied in practice because we will always lack precise measurement of the future value of many activities, two obvious examples being advertising, and research and development.

Time discounting would seem to be the most obvious aspect of the principle of alternate opportunity if we did not observe so many ways in which it is ignored in the making of business decisions. We all recognize the principle—a dollar today is worth more than the same dollar later. It is usually stated the other way around: a future dollar is worth less than a current one, how much less being dependent on the length of time and on the discount rate we apply. There are two obvious reasons. A dollar, like a bird, in hand is more certain than one in the bush; time is the principal ingredient of uncertainty. In addition, we could find some alternate productive use for the dollar while we were waiting. This alternate use is what determines the proper discount rate, the i in the basic formula:

$$V = \frac{R_n}{(1 + i)^n}$$

Where:

V = discounted present value

R_n = the actual return to be received at some future specific time

i = the rate of interest

n = the number of interest periods

Note that discounting works both ways: both future income and future costs are less. Where costs are spread over time, there is, of course, a series of calculations—one for each period in which the cost or revenue is due. Fortunately, conveniently calculated tables of present value are readily available.

The most important application of the discounting principle is in the making of investment decisions, in capital budgeting. But it obviously applies whenever either costs or returns are spread over time, as in some kinds of advertising investment, in the training of employees, or in spending for research and development, for example.

The time perspective of a decision is an important determinant of what should be measured in costs, revenues, and profits; it is the distinction between the economist's short-run and long-run. The economist defines these terms very precisely. A decision is short-run if some of the resource inputs must be considered as fixed for the purpose of decision. A decision to add a second shift to a one-shift operation is a good example in which costs may be viewed from a short-run standpoint (no added plant construction costs are incurred). Any decision which must consider all costs as variable is, by definition, a decision for the long-run. Such would be a decision to build a new plant, for instance. Short-run costs are thus those which, in the framework of the decision faced, are escapable; long-run costs assume no relevant cost is escapable in the ultimate.

From the standpoint of practice, the kinds of costs that will vary and the amount of variation is almost a continuum; there are shorter and longer varieties of the short-run. In every decision, then, some evaluation must be made as to which costs can be forecast as variable and thus escapable, and which fixed and inescapable, for the purpose of that decision. Such forecasts are not always easy, which means that the costing decision is often far from routine.

The Practical Art of the Forecast

A decision implies a forecast, i.e., some specific expectation of the outcome of that decision, based on some kind of assumed model as to the way this result will come about. The decision will be a wiser one if the forecasting is explicit and conscious and done with a clear understanding of the rules and arts of forecasting, of probability in its broadest sense, and of the need for carefully considered forecast models.

MODELS AND FORECASTING

Model has become an academically fashionable word in recent years for the sound reason that the term describes more accurately the ideas we used to express by a whole group of hard-to-separate terms: theory, hypothesis, law, hunch, etc. The meaning, when stripped of its obfuscating aura of the mystical, is quite simply that of the picture we have in our minds of the relationships between some kind of hoped for or feared outcome and some group of factors we think will bring the end about. This picture may be expressible in some mathematical shorthand which can be conveniently computerized. But it need not be so expressible in mathematical form, and for broad areas of scientific knowledge it is not. A model may be in the form of some kind of space conceptualizations, for example, like the Tinkertoy structural formulas that have opened up the marvelous world of synthetic organic chemistry, or some other positional or hierarchical relationship like the ecological models described by such concepts as predator, prey, symbiosis, etc., with which the economic biologist explains the growth and decline of different species in a given environment. A model may be the chart patterns of the Dow theorist, the weather front and storm path models of the weather forecaster, or the theology underlying the rain dance rituals of the Indians of the Southwest.

A model, in other words, is simply a consciously or unconsciously held conclusion in this form: "If I do this (or if _____ occurs), then I can *expect* that _____ will happen." Note the emphasis on *expect*. The fact that rain does not always follow the rain dance does not destroy faith in the ritual, and if the railroads confirm but the market turn proves abortive, the Dow theorist does not abandon his graphics. In both cases, the explanation is that other factors intervened. We recognize our models as simplifications of a reality too complex for direct comprehension. We attempt to account for only those factors we consider major and intentionally ignore others considered to be *individually* of much less importance, or which are presumed to exist but are unknown.

Anyone who makes a forecast of any kind—which means anyone who makes any decision about a future course of action—uses some kind of model of relationships about elements in that situation, whether or not he is aware that he is assuming some model.

When a bus line asks for a 5 percent hike in rates, it is assuming a quantitative model of the relationship of price and traffic such that the anticipated drop in riders will be more than offset by the rise in fare per rider, i.e., the familiar economic model of relatively inelastic demand. Otherwise, the fare increase request would make no sense. Similarly, when the President's advisors estimate that a tax rate cut of $10 billion will result in an eventual increase in actual taxes of the order of $12 billion, they obviously have in mind a relatively precise model of the interaction of taxes, economic growth, and profits.

A drug manufacturer who spends all of his promotion money selling and advertising his ethical drugs to physicians, who are unlikely to be buyers in any significant volume, is using a structural model of the market which assumes that the actual buyers (the patients) and the wholesale buyers (the druggists) have no significant influence on their sale. In the main, he is right.

Some aspect of the model must be mathematical when the decision is a question of how much: how much cost, price, receipts, production, capacity, profit, or how much to spend. A very large majority of business decisions are basically questions of how much. But many decisions also require the specification of where or in what manner, and this part of the model must be structural.

Whether mathematical or structural, consciously used or unconsciously assumed, any model is of necessity a simplified representation of the actual future course of events. All minor factors cannot possibly be taken into account, and have to be treated as nonexistent because their *individual* significance is not measurable. But when, as sometimes happens, they do not cancel each other out to a great extent, their actual existence reveals to us that we have simplified. Patients *do* exert some pressure on the doctor to prescribe even very specific medicines at times, and the physician does give in to this pressure occasionally. But the net value of this factor does not justify the cost of taking account of it. The economist estimating the probable effect of a tax cut knows that the values of the multiplier and the accelerator, which he assumes, are neither stable nor really precise. But he also knows he cannot possibly anticipate all of the major choices that will be made by taxpayers when they find themselves with the additional funds, and that many other factors influencing economic events are unknowable in advance.

A model should thus be complex only to the degree needed to take into account those knowable factors likely to affect the average outcome to a significant degree. The model should be simple enough so that decision-making does not get bogged down either in the hunt for added data to take into account lesser variations, or in the calculation of intricate formulas, and it should make a clear distinction between the various levels of predictability of events.

EVALUATING THE LEVELS OF PREDICTABILITY

Forecasting is the art of analyzing what is known about the past in terms of its meaning for the future. The naive predict by simply extending the most recent trend and eventually are trapped by the inevitable turning of every trend. True, such a persistence forecast is better than an arbitrary guess; there is considerable inertia in the course of events. But the important aspect of forecasting is to catch the turns in advance. The existence of such turns and variations in trend is the nearest thing to certainty we have. Forecasting is the art of analyzing the forces underlying current trends to estimate how much we know about that future variability, and its extent. Our ability to do so will differ for different aspects of that future.

From a pragmatic point of view, factors and relationships affecting future events can be roughly divided into four main groups: the *near certainties,* the *calculable risks,* the *estimable uncertainties,* and the *really unknowable.* These groups are not separated by any sharp dividing line and in fact, even the general category depends partly on the background and skill of the forecaster.

The best information we have is only a *near certainty;* nothing is really certain about the future. Some people really do escape taxes. Death at some time may be inevitable, but its timing is the important question. But some relationships are so unlikely to vary that, as a practical matter, any reasonable discount applied to their probability will not greatly affect decision.

Business decision can be greatly aided by paying close attention to some of the common, highly repetitive, near certainties. *Seasonal patterns,* for example, are a very widespread and often very stable phenomenon. Even industries with widely fluctuating year-to-year sales will exhibit remarkably undeviating proportions of sales volume within the year because of habitual customer purchase patterns or as a direct result of climatic patterns. Other industries will have a clearly defined *cyclical pattern* because of the normal life of items used, or of the reaction of price and profit expectations on plans and the existence of a clear gestation period such as the corn-hog ratio and pork production cycle. While *fashion cycles* do not have as clear periodicity as these others, they permeate far more of our culture than is generally realized, and their trend can be observed and turns anticipated by careful analysis. There is nothing more certain than that they *will* change.

Other types of near certainty derive directly from our knowledge of the present. This is especially true for many phenomena based on population changes. The pattern of death and survival, by age and sex, in the mass, within a given country, is quite stable and predictable. Knowing no more than this pattern and the current population, we can, for example, project the college population for 18-20 years ahead and the composition of the working population.

Calculable risks comprise that class of events that are not very predictable individually, but highly regular of occurrence in the mass. The longevity of any given individual is not very predictable, but in the mass of several hundred individuals the predictability becomes high enough to form the basis of one of our more profitable industries, insurance. Many of the events impinging on business success fall into the class of calculable risks, e.g., such population factors as births, deaths, marriages, divorces and such competitive factors as the certain entry of competition when profit margins are obviously high.

The *estimable uncertainties,* and their quantification, are probably the least widely understood aspect of forecasting. This comprises that class of expected occurrences about the general likelihood of which we feel we know something, but whose probability is largely a matter of personal opinion based on very limited or analogous information and largely unarticulated personal experience. Any nonduplicated individual expected event falls in this class, and thus do most of the really crucial business decisions. Although the probability values necessary to weigh their importance cannot be found in any experience table, an executive with real experience can usually assign some *relative order of value* to the uncertainty involved, a value not wholly irrelevant nor merely a guess. Proper evaluation of such *subjective probabilities* and of their validity should be a part of every careful forecast, as for example, the estimate of the probable reaction of individual competitors to the introduction of a radical new product by the firm, or to a change in its price structure.

Every forecaster must, finally, make some estimate of the *extent of the influence of the unknowable* in order to arrive at an overall estimate of the accuracy of his forecast. It is the certainty of the existence of unknowable factors that renders forecasting an art and at the same time makes careful estimation of it necessary to the essential quantification of the whole.

What Kind of Profit Do We Maximize?

So far, we have purposely avoided any definition of profit—a word with many possible interpretations. Profit is a type of concept the future value of which will always be a rough approximation, since it is a residual and thus subject to the cumulative error of every estimate entering a business calculation. In addition, there is a very real question as to whether any of the measures of management's immediate objectives are really closely related to profit in any sense.

The most common management objective, apparently, is total sales or total market share, which may not be closely correlated to profit. But whatever the actual relationship in any given case, there can be little question that these measures are used because they seem unambiguous, and because they are *believed* to be closely related to profit. Nor can there be much question that there is, in general, some relationship, and that profits themselves are hard to estimate for the future and not always easy to define for the past.

Even for current and past costs, the problems of allocation of joint costs and depreciation leave such room for ambiguity that equally competent accountants can come up with contradictory figures. In addition, the accounting rules they use for short-run appraisal are not likely to meet the need for the kind of profit estimate required for wise forward planning.

For forward planning, management usually is interested, even if unconsciously, in a single concept of profit measurement: the *discounted expected value* of the residual future income flows expected to result from the execution of a decision, after meeting all costs of carrying it out. *All* of the long-run effects on income flow must be considered, since the firm normally expects to stay in business indefinitely. For example, present income can not be at the expense of customer goodwill in the future, or unwelcome government regulation. The income flows forecast must be discounted for their timing, and the estimate reduced by the expected degree of uncertainty.

Profit so defined cannot really be estimated accurately. This definition has three corollaries:

1. The realized profit will coincide with the estimate only by coincidence. The final entries will not show the time discount, nor reflect the initial probabilities of their realization.

2. Some of the profits will lie in the avoidance of indirect losses of a different character. A firm may really optimize profits by taking less immediate return than it could, for example, because it hopes to save markets it would lose, develop new ones needed later, relieve pressures in upcoming wage negotiations, or avoid threatening legal interference and guarantee its otherwise unhampered existence. All of these have a monetary value, if successful, but the precise amount of value can rarely be pinpointed.

3. Since the estimate itself is a *probable* or *expected value*, what we have estimated is a range of possible values of a series of different decisions made in a similar manner on the basis of the same kind of information. In any individual case, some shortfall or overestimate is quite likely.

This work assumes, in other words, that one aim of a firm is to maximize the profitability of its operations over an indefinitely long life, as it appears to the firm's management. The method proposed is the quantification of the six value concepts outlined in this chapter, making full analytical use of every kind of available information with quantity implications of any level. Some of the better tools for getting meaning out of such data are discussed next.

Summary

1. Managerial economics seeks to provide guides for the forecasting of opportunities for profit. Good forecasting of any sort requires some basic *model* of the mechanisms by which the actions decided upon can be expected to produce an expected outcome, carefully defined *concepts* of the factors involved in this model of relationships, and some *yardsticks* for determining the values to be fitted into these concepts.

2. The basic model for business decision is that of monopolistic competition, broadly defined to include what some refer to separately as differentiated oligopoly. This model rests on five basic postulates: (a) *Any product* is a bundle of psychological satisfactions or services, and each element in the bundle has a different value for different buyers. (b) Successful bundles contain some specific *differential element* of high value to some specific market segment, and thus partake of monopoly. Other market segments place little or no value on this differential element, and for these fringe segments, the seller is in competition with sellers of other products. (c) *Product* and *price* are *intertwined* variables in business decision. The primary aim of the seller is to establish a *differential advantage* in some segment of the market by means of a product-price combination at which he excels. (d) Management acts in the knowledge that *its acts influence the acts of others.* (e) Since product characteristics are more difficult to parallel than price structures, *management strategy tends to focus on product differentiation* and to accept the limitations on price structure established by trade practice and consumer reaction.

This model focusses on innovation in physical product and marketing practice as the principal source of profit. The central role of innovation rules out set solutions and makes of decision a process of probability forecasting.

3. The basic economic value *concepts* in this model are:

> *demand* (and its mirror image, *supply*) defined as willingness to sacrifice something of value in exchange for some of the services offered in the seller's bundle. Some of these services may be embodied in the physical form of the product, some merely associated with its purchase
>
> *production* as the creation of desired value, by any means
>
> *competition* as a many-sided phenomenon, with many products, and even many kinds of products, competing for the various market segments served by a producer, each according to the satisfaction mix bought by that segment
>
> *cost* as alternate opportunity cost
>
> *price* as the sacrifice of any sort which a customer willingly pays for a given satisfaction mix
>
> *capital investment* as the purchase of a series of income flows, its value determined by the discounted probable value of those flows.

4. The basic *yardstick* for determination of the value of any of these factors is alternate opportunity in its various aspects of *incrementalism, marginalism, equimarginalism,* and *time discounting,* measured in terms of the *time perspective* of the decision under consideration.

5. Since every decision implies a forecast, the manager needs to understand that any forecast rests on some kind of model of the situation, and must take into account data of four levels of predictability.

6. A model is simply a conceptual image of the mechanism by which an outcome is expected to come about. It may be expressible in mathematical form, or be a concept of the structure of elements in a situation. Since business decision must result in a very specific quantitative commitment of resources, some aspect of the model must express quantitative relationships. And since

the where and in what manner of decision is also important, it must have some structural aspects.

7. For the purpose of forecasting, events may be divided into four general levels of foreseeability: near certainties, calculable risks, estimable uncertainties, and the unknowable.

8. The manager needs to be aware of the *near certainties*. There are a number of such patterns in business capable of shedding considerable light on the future. Knowledge of stable seasonal patterns permits the early forecasting of the near future events from initial events early in a year. Some industries have reasonably regular cyclical patterns. Awareness of fashion cycles can prepare a firm for inevitable turn-arounds in taste. The future of many aspects of population composition important to many businesses is implicit for many years ahead in the current population composition.

9. *Calculable risks* are usually recognized as such by business. These include events that are individually relatively unpredictable, but are repetitive and relatively stable in the mass.

10. *Estimable uncertainties* include one-time events and others about which we do not have enough experience to make a certain calculation, but about whose likelihood we can make a subjective estimate that is better than an arbitrary guess.

11. Any forecast must include some assessment of the extent to which *unknowable factors* influence the outcome.

12. In this book, the subject of forecasting is profit, defined as the discounted probable value of future income flows expected to be added as a result of a decision, over the long run. This really means we are talking about a goal the attainment of which can not be checked, even after the fact.

2

Pinpointing the "How Much" of a Decision

CONCEPTS WITHOUT specific figures are no guide to successful action. All business decision, in the end, hinges on a single question: "*How much* would I have to put in, and precisely *how much* can I expect to get out?" Both the input and the expected output have to be expressed in very specific sets of figures. Those figures must be valid in relation to the decision being made. They must fit the concepts as they would be defined in reference to that particular decision, and those who use them must be familiar with both their real significance and their limitations. The manager can delegate the calculations used to draw the hidden meaning out of the raw data *if* he understands the nature of the tools being used. But he cannot delegate judgment of their meaning for his decision without abdicating his responsibility for that decision. He must know the figures he uses and their precise significance for the action being considered. He must also translate what he knows and feels about the uncertainties in the situation into a specific quantity statement if he is to properly judge alternatives with different levels of risk.

Determining the crucial *how much* of a decision thus requires four kinds of understanding:

1. knowledge of the precise significance of the figures being used, for the purpose intended
2. comprehension of the necessity for and methods of putting a

specific value on the subjective and objective uncertainties in the situation

3. familiarity with the capabilities of the mathematical tools available for revealing the hidden forces operating to produce observed results
4. a grasp of the useful characteristics of the mathematical devices for estimation of the optimum values to be sought or used.

Knowing the Figures You Use

The figures used to evaluate alternatives for decisions must be as critically examined as the amounts on the checks issued to carry out the decision and the validity of the checks to be received as a result of it. Unfortunately, figures and mathematical symbolism tend to be viewed as forms of black magic by far too many people, with the result that either close examination is shunned, or their mystical intricacies are delightedly sought. Both attitudes deprive the manager of the clear focus he needs on the *how much* of decision.

Figures possess no inherent magic. They are simply a device for compressing the quantitative aspect of what we know into small enough compass for ready comprehension and investigation of its corollaries. Figures neither confer meaning nor add to it; they simply help us understand whatever meaning there is to start with, if any. Determining whether there is any meaning at all, and what it is, is the first step toward wise quantitative analysis. The decision maker must do this himself. He cannot leave the evaluation of the significance up to the cost accountant, EDP expert, or other technician less familiar with the purpose of their use; to do so is to delegate the decision itself. The manager need not be an accountant to evaluate the logic of cost estimates nor a computer programmer to assess the meaning of a linear program calculation.

The key to the meaning of quantitative information lies in the answer to five simple questions:

1. Where did the figures come from?
2. Where and how are they to be used?

3. How consistent are they internally and with what might be expected?
4. If expressed in the form of rates or other summary parameters, is this the correct way to use them for the purpose of the decision?
5. If decision hinges in any way on trends revealed in the data, how persistent are the forces underlying the trends?

Answering these questions requires no CPA, nor Ph.D. in mathematics, but something much rarer—painstaking examination of the data and its origins.

A figure is only a simplified representation of some events or states of nature. Whatever meaning it has derives from the analogy between these events and states and the end result sought by decision. If the data refer to the cost of producing runs of 250,000 widgimatic subassemblies, we must know under what assumptions of capacity, tooling, labor, and other relevant conditions these figures are derived. If the cost contains some kinds of allocations for fixed, joint, and programmed costs, we must know how each item in the aggregate allocation is arrived at and is included, and why, and their actual relation to the production of any size of run of these subassemblies. Once we have determined this much we are ready to ask the second question—the purpose for which these figures are going to be used.

However much we know about where our figures come from, we still must look very closely at what they are going to be used for before we can pronounce them meaningful. Data that is quite useful in the context for which it is normally gathered may be quite misleading if used as is for the purpose of decision. This is especially true of rule-of-thumb calculations widely used in business record-keeping. Allocated costs are a prime example. For routine accounting purposes, these usually serve a quite necessary control purpose in keeping track of the relative profitability of various parts of the enterprise. But for decisions involving substantial change in the size, direction, or nature of activity, they may include quite irrelevant items or lead to double counting of costs, or both. They may even omit relevant costs. An overhead allocation percentage may include a substantial tooling cost, for example. If the decision requires a major increase in production level, we cannot add any needed new tooling cost to costs figured using the previous allocation percentage. We will be adding in part of our tooling cost twice. Or if a new operation uses less tooling, or a lower level of production is planned, tooling items in that overhead calculation must come out.

Likewise, the company must carry depreciation on its books in terms of its meaning for taxation purposes. But this is not necessarily the level of depreciation cost that should be charged against a specific production decision to determine the economic profit yielded by a given price. And since depreciation includes some of the longer run wear and tear as a component, to add wear-and-tear cost to a specific job would be double counting.

Double counting of costs, and omission of real imputed costs, is very easy at the decision level because most of the figures used are conglomerations of a number of calculations added into some summary quantity. Two ways of staying on the alert for possible miscalculations is to compare figures for their internal consistencies and for their correspondence with what you normally would expect them to look like. If, for example, in adding up the directly measurable incremental costs of two proposed alternatives, the costs come out different from the total costs for each of the two estimates when all calculations are included, then a close scrutiny of all items in both calculations is called for. If cost estimates for large runs seem to be little less than for small runs, or are even more, this unexpected result certainly needs questioning. And if a price change is not estimated to result in a different demand pattern, we should usually ask why not.

Percentages, rates, and averages are powerful tools to aid us in making and comprehending the kinds of comparisons needed to reveal the relative worth of our alternate opportunities. When they are used for the static comparison of quantities arrived at by other means, there is no harm in using such condensed parameters in a way not intended by their mathematical implications. But they do imply relationships that may not be true if the rates are used against a changed set of data. Thus, a percentage or any other rate implies a straight line proportionate relationship if used to estimate quantities at a different level than that used as the base of calculation. If used in cost calculations, for example, they imply that all costs so calculated are directly and continuously variable with the level of production. Before any rate is used to make a forecast, every significant element entering into its original estimate should thus be examined to make sure that the assumption of continuous straight-line variability is a reasonable approximation.

Probably no other type of data is so widely misinterpreted as that including trends. Much too commonly, the naive assumption is made that the trend will continue indefinitely, or at least beyond the period involved in the decision to be made. Yet it will be hard to find a trend of any kind in our fluctuating world which has not experienced some kind of temporary reversal, and most of them have major turning points sooner or later. This is especially true of nearly every phenomenon important to costs and profits. Indeed, by far the most important element in profit making is foreseeing the turning point and direction of trends, and their timing, before they become obvious to everyone else. A long continued trend is more likely to be one nearing the end of its course than one that is likely to continue. To determine which, it is always necessary to analyze the forces that made for the trend and to estimate the amount of life left in them, i.e., to go behind the trend itself to the underlying reasons for it. Some hint as to the imminence of change can be had by examining some of the details associated with the trend, however. Most turning points are preceded by hints of a slowdown in some aspect of the trend. The profit rate for new expansion in a booming industry begins to fall below target. Daily gains in a booming stock market tend to be less, the reactions more violent. Seasonal patterns not previously evident begin to be pronounced. And so on. A detailed examination of the various figures involved in the trend will usually reveal one of these warning hints. But such empirical hints can be false signals if not accompanied by an analysis of the forces causing the boom and the current state of their health.

In sum, every business decision of any sort is based on either implied quantities or explicit figures. We must know these figures and be able to establish their relevance for the purpose of this decision. We can do this only when we know how they were generated in the first place and how this affects their meaning for the use intended, and have checked their internal consistency and whether or not they look right in terms of what we would expect. If some of them are expressed as rates, we must be sure that this is the right way to use them for our forecast purpose. If some of them reveal trends, and these trends are an element in our decision, we must make a carefully considered judgment as to the probable persistence of the trends and the probable timing of any turning points by an analysis of the forces responsible for the trend.

Not until we have done our analytical homework on available figures are we ready for the second step in quantitative analysis: application of an uncertainty discount to estimate the investment value of a necessarily speculative venture.

Discounting for the Subjectively Estimated Degree of Uncertainty

The uncertainties being faced in any given decision seldom have equal associated levels of risk and uncertainty. "Don't count your chickens before they are hatched" is an old barnyard adage with direct application to decision when understood in its original context. Any well-run farm always counted the chickens expected from a hatch when the eggs were set. *But the informed farmer expected less chicks than eggs put to hatch,* and made additional allowances for later losses from disease and predators. So must the business manager reduce his estimates by some hatching percentage—here referred to as an *uncertainty discount*—to permit valid comparison of alternatives with different associated levels of uncertainty.

Outcomes, e.g., revenue, sales, costs, of any proposed decision are properly estimated as the product of three quantities: (1) the best estimate of the actual outcome expected, (2) the time discount percentage, and (3) the estimated probability of occurrence of the particular amount expected. Time discounting has already been touched on, and is widely, although not universally, used. But few managements apply a carefully considered uncertainty discount to the estimates used. Rather, the tendency often is to present estimates under the most optimistic assumptions and *then* argue, if at all, about their absolute level. As a result, projects may be adopted with estimates taking insufficient account of foreseeable uncertainties because the optimists win out. Or projects with a good chance of probable profit may be abandoned because pessimists throw up too heavy a cloud of doubt on the absolute value of estimated costs and revenues. Arguments tend toward the " 'tain't true—'tis so true" level rather than toward a mutual attempt to narrow down opposing estimates of probability by joint examination of available information and experience.

Yet, in the context of objectively determinable probabilities, management has no trouble understanding the uncertainty discount. If faced with two alternatives with known experience records, e.g., one known to succeed 80 percent of the time, the other just 40 percent of the time, management unhesitatingly insists on a proportionately higher payout under the insurance, or risk principle.

This same uncertainty discount principle is valid when applied to the subjectively estimated uncertainties of the more important decisions concerning unique operations—those for which no precisely similar risk experience is available, but about which a rough estimate of the degree of uncertainty can be estimated subjectively through use of background knowledge, analogy, and logical analysis.

HOW IS THE UNCERTAINTY DISCOUNT APPLIED?

Let us look at the uncertainty discount in a fictitious example. Your attention, as president of NG Chemicals, has been called to a lively growing demand in the West Coast market for your new wonder plastic resin, barsillium, to the capacity operation of competitor's plants there, and to the freight disadvantage you now have in serving this lush market. Production has proposed building a Los Angeles plant. They point to the relatively high profit the barsillium operation is bringing in and project the rate of growth in sales on the basis of the current trend. They have drawn up a tentative plan for a 20 million dollar, 20 million pound capacity plant and they estimate a discounted return of 14 percent after taxes, using a ten year life and straight line depreciation.

This is much better than the present average of 10 percent on all of the firm's business.

But a number of members of the Executive Committee object. They say not enough attention has been paid to some negative factors:

1. If the market continues to grow as projected, Southern and Northern California competitors with existing plants and space for expansion may take up the slack.

2. Barsillium competes directly in some market uses with two older resins made by competitors, antonium and brutonium, which are currently price depressed because of excess capacity. At present barsillium is more expensive even after due allowance is made for the greater yield of barsillium. Present barsillium sales have come from market segments in which it has a marked performance advantage over these two, but most future growth must be in uses in which the competition is more direct. For 25 cents a pound capacity less than the cost of building new barsillium capacity, antonium and brutonium capacity can be converted. The objectors believe the present price of barsillium will have to drop in the near future, and also that some of the excess antonium and brutonium capacity will be converted.

3. Opponents also think the construction cost estimates are somewhat low. They remind the president that the last two facilities built ran 5 percent and 7 percent above original careful, calculated estimates, due to selective materials price increases and increased labor rates.

Proponents admit that there is always some uncertainty in business, but insist that the objections are all pure speculation, and point to the uniformly profitable record of all expansion in recent years. Opponents object, however, that this is a new kind of expansion, into a more competitive situation than any planned before.

Which side is right? On this absolute basis, neither one. Neither the cost and profit estimates of the plant proponents nor the problems foreseen by the opponents are fully sustainable. The objections have no figures tied to them at this point, and until this is done, proper allowance for the risks expected cannot be calculated. Some agreed-upon estimates must be made of the probability of occurrence of price changes, plant conversion, and competitor expansion, and of an expanded demand for barsillium on the West Coast. Let us see how the plant capacity estimates might work out.

Assuming no change in the relative prices of barsillium and the two older resins, the sales department estimates that the 1965 total sales of all companies in this market of 50 million pounds will increase to 80 million by 1967, which is the earliest a completely new plant can be in production, and to 95 million pounds by 1968. The present market is divided as follows:

(In millions of pounds)
Total 50

West Coast producers		Outside sources	
Able Chemical Co.	12.5	NG Chemicals	5
Beta Corporation	15	Others	17.5
Others	none		

Able Chemicals is an aggressive, growing resin producer, with a strong regional sales force and is ambitious to strengthen its share of market. Beta is a conservative subsidiary of another Eastern corporation. In the opinion of NG executives, it will expand only as it needs to hold on to its dominant share of the market. Both also produce antonium and brutonium. In addition, there are five other West Coast producers of these two older resins with a total resin capacity of 110 million pounds, which have not entered the barsillium market. Conversion of any of this would take a year.

No firm has announced any plans for expansion or conversion of capacity as yet, but the Able Company is considered almost certain to be planning at least a 10 million pound plant, on the basis of the estimated market expansion and their known desire to increase their foothold. In addition, after consideration of the probable demands of Able customers, the greater profitability of barsillium, and the general ambitions of its management, NG officials believe there is a lesser, but not negligible, probability their sights may be set even higher than this. After some discussion, they arrive at the following estimate of probabilities in the case of Able expansion and conversion:

	Added Capacity (ΔC) (In millions of pounds)		Prob- ability (P)		Probable realiza- tion (P x ΔC)
1967	10		.99		10
	2		.4		.8
	3		.33		1
	5	(conversion)	.2		1
				TOTAL	12.8
1968	5	(conversion)	.25		1.25

Probable 1967 capacity: 25 million pounds   *1968:* 27 million pounds
(Note that totals are rounded off to reflect the approximation involved.)

The 1968 conversion probability depends on Able's achieving a doubling of its sales of barsillium and the continuation of its relative profitability, so the chances are considered only one in four.

From what is known about Beta management, it is unlikely that it will consider expansion until pressed for deliveries, probably in 1966. They would then plan to build enough, normally, to meet commitments, and perhaps a little more, but not much, since they like to operate close to capacity. For Beta, the estimate finally arrived at is:

	(ΔC) (In millions of pounds)	(P)		(P x ΔC)
1968:	12	.99		12
	5	.75		4
	5	.2		1
			TOTAL	17

Considering their relative market positions and sales organizations, the other five producers of the older resins are also thought likely to convert considerable capacity in 1967 and some more in 1968. The probability, calculated as for the others, leads to an expected total for the five together, in 1967, of 16 million pounds of added capacity, and 6 million more in 1968. West Coast construction by the other outside suppliers is not considered very probable at this time, so that the total expected local capacity for the near future projects as follows:

| | (In millions of pounds) | | |
	1965	1967	1968
TOTAL	27.5	76	101
NG	—	20	20
Able	12.5	25	27
Beta	15	15	32
Others	—	16	22
Estimated local sales	50	80	95

Thus local capacity, if NG builds the plant, will be nearly enough to take care of the local market at the time of plant completion and in excess, according to the best estimate, within a year afterward. But this does not take into consideration the practical certainty that the outside producers will fight to maintain at least their current share of market. Thus there is almost certain to be a pressure of supplies on the market by the time the plant could be completed. This, in turn, raises questions about the assumptions concerning prices, and also concerning the use of straight-line ten year depreciation.

It is apparent that the entire calculation needs to be recast in the face of these expectations. It may, of course, when all other opportunities are evaluated, still look like a good investment.

ARE SUBJECTIVE PROBABILITIES A USEFUL BASIS FOR ESTIMATE?

The above example is like most such business decisions in that it deals with a single event for which there is no possible directly applicable experience. The risk involved is not calculable on the basis of some tabulation of really similar past events. It is a figure put on subjective estimates that are not arbitrary guesses, but reasoning based on observations of the actions of people involved in somewhat analogous situations in the past, or on other relevant information. They do not predict, as does a true objective probability, the number of times the expected events *will* occur in a large number of truly similar events, since the events foreseen are unique, and unlikely to be repeated in the future. Further, what does happen in actuality is not likely to look too much like the resulting estimate. The single event has only two real probabilities: either it happens $(P = 1)$ or it does not $(P = 0)$. Able will either build a minimum size plant, or it will not. It will not build a half-size plant.

Is it legitimate to use such figures in the manner illustrated? *No,* if they are really arbitrary guesses without basis in some kind of knowledge applicable to the situation, or if they are emotional reactions based on wish fulfillment, and if they are not checked up on afterward to improve future estimating procedures. *Yes,* if they are careful logical constructions based on personal observations and impressions of those in a position to know, with perhaps the addition of some studies of the market factors that can be expected to affect matters, all considered in as cold an objective light as is possible; and if it is clearly kept in mind that these are very rough approximations, and they are treated as such. If treated in this manner, they differ from the more objective types of probabilities we are more used to only in the kind of knowledge on which the estimate is based.

All statements of probability are simply estimates of the extent to which our knowledge of possible future events is applicable. The very stable probabilities used by the insurance actuary to estimate your remaining life expectancy are not a statement of fact in your individual case. It is solely a prediction based on what is known about the mortality experience of men in the past who were similar to you only in the four characteristics of age, sex, occupation, and country of residence, and also in that they enjoyed a certain minimum level of health. Insurers will make a firm contractual commitment to contribute to your estate because they have reason to believe that in the long run, in the sum of thousands of such commitments to various individuals, they will reach an *average expected payout*. The insurance companies have no knowledge of how well any individual contract will pay out and would be surprised if the average were extremely close to actual in a large majority of the cases.

When we have a backlog of dependable experience covering a few of the major common factors in a situation, and when we are dealing with repetitive events with the same common major factors, we call our prediction an *objective probability* and speak of the uncertainty as a mere *insurable risk*. But when we are concerned about the outcome of a single event, e.g., your own real life expectancy, there is no difference between such risks and other types of uncertainties about which some estimate can be made. In neither case can we say anything for certain about the individual outcome or its payout. In both cases, we can make some statement of the expected payout with long-run validity for decisions taken in the light of the same amount and kind of knowledge. While the calculation of the uncertainty discount does not reveal the eventual actual payout except by coincidence, it does permit the comparison of different alternatives with different attached uncertainties, making use of all knowledge bearing on the proposed alternatives. This is its real purpose.

If some of this information lends itself to some objective statement of probability for some aspect, so much the better. In addition, we have tools that can bring out such objective knowledge.

Analyzing for the Basic Forces Hidden Under the Detail

Raw figures, like rough diamonds and most valuable ores, do not reveal their full value to the casual glance. This value is brought out only by skillful processing with the right tools. Once the existence of values has been confirmed by critical analysis of their relevance to the action considered, there are three general classes of mathematical tools for extracting the significance hidden in our figures. Roughly in the order of their usefulness, these major tools are:

1. frequency distribution analysis as a guide to hidden possibilities
2. trend analysis to reveal underlying factors operating over time
3. Markov chain analysis to indicate the nature of probabilities

underlying a dynamic situation and to estimate their end point, and its timing.

SUBMERGING THE DETAILS TO DISCOVER THE PATTERNS: FREQUENCY ANALYSIS

The most powerful and most widely applicable tools are fortunately nearly always the most simple. The diamond cutter turns a rough-looking pebble into a brilliant ornament with little more than a small hammer and a wedge. With much business data, the most revealing mathematical procedure is simply to look at it in an ordered mass, i.e., in some form of frequency distribution. As a forest can be comprehended only by backing off from the individual trees and underbrush to gain perspective on the whole, so business data takes on a different significance when individual figures are seen in the mass.

Frequency distribution analysis and trend analysis can be powerful devices for achieving this focus on the overall meaning. Frequency distribution analysis takes little more mathematical equipment than a pair of perceptive eyes and the ability to draw simple graphs or bar charts. There are three basic tools of frequency curve analysis:

1. use of cumulative frequencies as an approximation of probabilities
2. normal curve analysis to signal the presence of constraining or disturbing factors
3. comparison of related distributions to highlight important characteristics of one or both.

Frequency Experience as a Set of Probabilities. Anyone who does any kind of forecasting develops some habitual patterns of using his figures for the forecast. If the model used in making the forecast has a valid relationship to events, the forecasts will have some pattern of relationship to those events. Thus any cost estimator's results will tend to cluster around some bias with regard to cost subsequently experienced. Any firm in a business requiring bids is likely to develop a consistent pattern in the way it bids any one type of job. The result of this consistency is not a single figure, e.g., a tendency to bid at 10 percent under a cost as estimated by another firm, but a clustering around some such value, with an appreciable dispersion around the central value. The sales manager may have a feel of the market accurate enough so that his forecast of production needs may tend to average out close to actual, but with varying degrees in individual cases of deviation from the actual. Cases like this can be treated as empirical approximations of the variations and central values to be expected. Gaps in the data can be smoothed out by using cumulative values, starting at one end of the range and graphing the result as a cumulative curve, on which approximations can be obtained by interpolation, if necessary (see Figure 2-1, below).

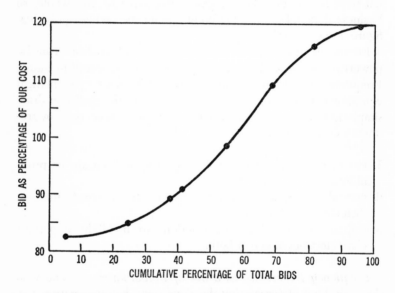

FIGURE 2-1. Past Record of Fox Corporation Submarplane Bids

The Normal Curve as a Yardstick for Expectations. Scientists have long known that a skilled observer with a single instrument making repeated observations of the same object or phenomenon will get, not one reading, but a series of different values which cluster around some central one in a bell-shaped distribution we

have come to call a *normal curve*. The central value exists because
the important factor determining his readings is the true measurement itself. The values vary because an infinity of individually
insignificant influences operate to distort the reading, cancelling
each other out partially or wholly at times, adding up to cause
extreme variation occasionally. Such a normal curve of error is to
be expected in any situation in which only one major factor influencing value is present and there is an infinity of "random"
insignificant influences to cause variation (and there nearly always is, in one form or another). Knowing this much, we have a
yardstick to check the possibility that a situation may contain
more than one element of important influence and also to assess
the strength of that dominant influence. The importance of the
normal curve lies in the signal, given by deviations from it, that
something new has entered the scene. This is the rationale of
statistical quality control. The occurrence of deviations outside
the control limits is a signal to seek something amiss in the process—something strong enough to bias the output.

But there is not one normal curve, but a whole family of them.
Some have the pleasantly plump bell shape we expect, as in
Figure 2-2 A (page 38), indicating nothing is happening to question our assumption that everything is under control. Others are
tall and stringy, as in Figure 2-2 B. This kind of squeezed-in bell
indicates that something is operating to hold variation within an
unnaturally tight limit. Such might be the distribution of the
proportions of a class failing in a school in which the principal in-
sisted that students should be passed regardless, or of the output
of a bricklayer crew if there was a tacit agreement on a day's work
as 495 bricks.

Some normal curves get flattened and sprawled out as in Figure
2-2 C. Such a distribution suggests a very weak dominant factor.
If this were the distribution of your cost estimates against realization, for example, you would want to tighten up your estimating
procedures.

The normal curve also tells us much about the great majority of
frequency distributions that are not bell-shaped. Thus, a curve
with two sharply defined humps as in Figure 2-2 D can be viewed
as the sum of two overlapping normal curves, as indicated by
the broken line projections. We would get such a distribution in

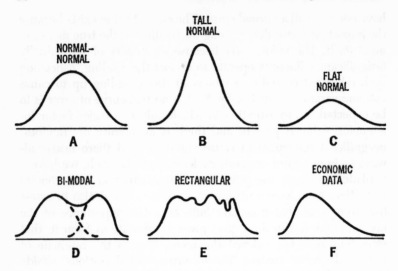

FIGURE 2-2. Some Variations of the Normal Curve and Three Other Distributions

a situation dominated by two different major factors. Of course, a distribution can have three such *modal points*. But if events are shaped by more than two or three major forces, we are likely to get the so-called *rectangular distribution* depicted in Figure 2-2 E. In such a situation, so many factors are at work that no one or two can be considered dominant. If this were the distribution of the quality of your factory output, your process would be considered completely out of control. If this were the distribution of the sizes and types being bought, we should probably conclude that tastes for this item were so diverse that only customized production is justified.

The most significant distribution for economic analysis is the highly skewed pattern of Figure 2-2 F, one bearing no recognizable resemblance to the normal curve. Peter Drucker refers to this as the *normal curve of social phenomena* [1] to distinguish it from the normal curve of measurement of natural events.

[1] Peter F. Drucker, *Managing for Results* (New York, Harper & Row, Publishers, 1964), pp. 8-10.

This curve is sometimes called the "90-10 principle," highlighting the almost universal economic tendency for a very large number, often 90%, of the effects to come from a very small concentration of the events—often 10%: 90% of the order volume from 10% of the customers, 90% of the consumption from 10% of the users, 90% of the costs from 10% of the activities, 90% of the profit from 10% of the items sold. The actual proportions are seldom exactly 90% and 10% of course—may be 70% and 30%, for instance.

Economic management must focus on the identification of these concentrations and work with them.

Discovery of Meaning by the Comparison of Distributions. Whatever the shape of the distribution, much can sometimes be revealed by cross-comparison with another distribution that is expected to be similar. For example, when a mail order merchandise buyer wanted to know why he had little success in promoting the sale of women's sportswear, a comparison of sports-

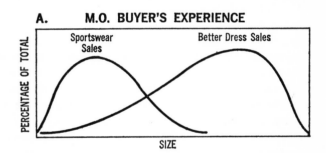

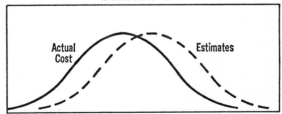

FIGURE 2-3. Two Distribution Comparisons

wear sales volume by size was made with the frequency distribution of the relatively satisfactory sales volume of better dresses by size, with the results about as sketched in Figure 2-3 (page 39). Similarly, an executive who became interested in trying to understand why his firm was relatively unsuccessful in landing bids on a type of work for which it was well qualified made a comparison of the frequency distribution of the company's cost estimates with actual costs realized later and got the distribution shown in Figure 2-3 B. The difference in the median bid and median actual cost was 5 percent. They had also been losing out on bids by an average of about 5 percent.

LOOKING BEYOND THE DETAIL FOR TRENDS

Most frequency distribution analysis disregards the time element, arranging the figures used in order of size. But the chronology itself is often an important element for analysis, either being a major factor itself or, more usually, a measure of some other factor such as growth, maturation, or saturation. What seem like unexplainable fluctuations can be revealed to contain a strong trend element when data is ordered along the time dimension.

Trends are important in two ways. Riding along with the trend is often far more profitable than disregarding it, and few trends continue in one direction indefinitely without reverse. Getting warning of the turning point and estimating its timing can forestall serious losses or represent an opportunity for unusual profit to the one who can get in before the trend is obvious to everyone. For an example of the kind of illumination graphic analysis can throw on otherwise confusing individual figures, consider the following realistic series of daily quotation changes for one stock:

+ 2.37	− 1.12	− 1.88	− .88	+ 1.88	− 1.12	+ 1.50	+ .37
+ .50	− 1.00	+ 1.50	− .25	+ .37	− .25	+ 1.25	+ .63
−	+ 1.88	+ 1.63	+ 1.12	+ 2.37	− .12	− .63	
− 1.00	+ .50	− 3.50	− 1.00	− 1.88	+ 1.37	+ 1.50	
− .25	+ .37	− 1.00	+ 1.50	+ .37	− 1.25	− .88	
+ .88	+ .63	− .37	+ 3.00	− .37	+ 1.00	+ .88	
− .62	+ 1.00	− 1.25	+ 1.00	+ .50	+ .12	− .75	
+ .62	+ .50	+ 1.63	− 1.50	− 2.12	+ .88	+ .75	

+	.37	− 1.25	−	.63	−	.88	− 1.63	− 1.63	−	.88
− 1.50	+ 1.37	+ 1.88	+	.88	+	.88	+ 2.00	+	.50
+ 1.25	+ 2.00	− 1.50	−	.88	−	.37	− 1.37	−	.75

How much pattern is visible here? Now look at the time graph of this same series (Figure 2-4, below). If you thought this pattern of fluctuations was going to persist, would you buy, or sell?

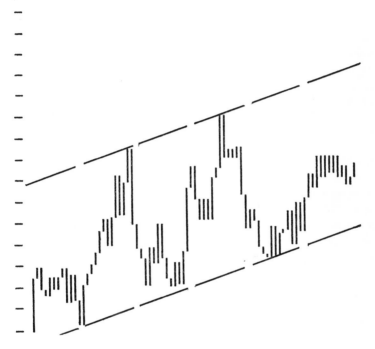

FIGURE 2-4. Time Graph

The ability of the time series graph to put variations in perspective of a trend, if any exists, is the reason every serious trader keeps or uses some kind of charting system. But note that the chart does not itself tell whether or not a trend will persist, or for how long. Nor does it note the *why* of the trend, and this latter is the kind of information needed to take advantage of the trend indicated—to forecast what will happen next. The answer to this lies outside the chart, but knowing the *when* and *how* of a trend shows the existence of some strong underlying force and helps narrow down the search for its identity, whether the fluctuation is in the price of a stock or in cost variances, or some other quantity important to business decision. In addition, changes in the intensity of the trend can foreshadow changes in direction and alert the manager to investigate the possibility.

Learning Curve Analysis—A Special Form of Trend Analysis. During World War II, the airframe industry discovered, and other industries are now learning, that a special kind of trend should be expected over the life of any process requiring the performance of a composite of many individual tasks. As the time period progressively doubles, the efficiency of any process improves at some

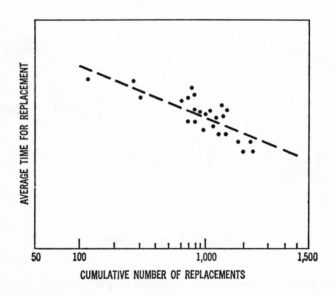

FIGURE 2-5. Maintenance Learning Curve at a General Electric Plant

Source: Carl A. Bennett, *Application of a Learning Curve to a Maintenance Problem* (Second Annual Quality Control Symposium of the Fort Worth-Dallas Section, ASQC, March 16, 1957).

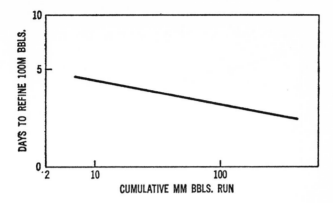

FIGURE 2-6. Performance Learning Curve of an Individual Fluid Catalytic Cracking Unit

Source: Winifred B. Hirschmann, "Profit From the Learning Curve," *Harvard Business Review*, Vol. 42, No. 1 (January-February, 1964), p. 130.

constant rate. If both time and efficiency are expressed in logarithms, we can plot the result as a straight line, with no turning point. This has come to be called, rather inaccurately, "the learning curve," and does result from one type of learning—the constant discovery of possible minor innovations in the process as men and engineers work with it over time. The actual rate of change is closely associated with the percentage of human activity required by the process, but such process improvement has been shown to happen even when the proportion of human activity is extremely limited, as in petroleum refining.[2]

Analysis of the trend in process efficiency thus gives management another yardstick. Since process improvement is the normal condition, its absence or diminished rate in comparison with the degree of human factor is a signal that something in the situation is inhibiting the normal process. That something may well lie in

[2] An excellent summary of learning curve theory and a well-illustrated discussion of its possibilities can be found in Winfred B. Hirschmann, "Profit from the Learning Curve," *Harvard Business Review*, Vol. 42, No. 1 (January-February, 1964), pp. 125 ff.

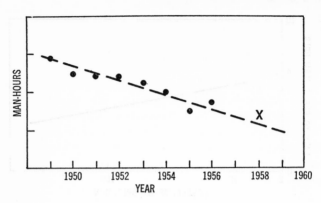

FIGURE 2-7. Learning Curve of Productive Refinery Labor Man-Hours for Maintenance and Shutdowns

management's own attitude at times. One discovery we have made is that whenever management puts no ceiling on the amount of process improvement it expects, the trend is continuous, but of course at a constantly diminishing straight-time rate as the process gets progressively older and more well established. Without question, the well and accurately publicized success of the Lincoln Electric Company is due almost entirely to management's deeply entrenched faith that progress is continuously possible, a faith that is communicated down to the person on the assembly line, and leads management itself to continuously look for ways of building progress incentive into its whole management structure.

These process improvement principles also add an element to the appraisal of investment alternatives. Since the rate of improvement is greatest in the early history of any process, costs will come down faster in new plants and new processes than in modernized old plants and processes. Thus where a new process seems to offer about the same return as the modernization of an old one, the new has hidden cost advantages that should be realized over time. The results of any process change should not be judged too hastily. Time should be allowed to let them prove their efficiency.

MATRIX ALGEBRA AND THE MARKOV CHAIN:
ESTIMATING THE FORCE UNDERLYING CHANGE

The assumption of the tedium of drawn-out calculations by the digital computer has brought into wide use a new form of algebraic symbolism known as matrix algebra. For a computer, this is a better form than the older style notation most are familiar with, and does much the same job. A matrix is nothing more than an unlabeled table with rows and columns of either figures *or* symbols, instead of lines of figures and symbols intermixed. If, for example, the simultaneous equations most of us worked with in high school are put into matrix form, the coefficients only are put into rows in the table, in the same order as in the equations we would recognize, and the variables are listed separately in a horizontal row or *vector* at the left of this table. Because of the different format, the rules for mechanical manipulation differ slightly, but the answers come out the same.

An interesting aspect of this notation is that any ordinary tabulation can also be looked at as a matrix to be solved. One potentially valuable application of this way of looking at a table concerns the use of a table that shows changes taking place during one time period as a basis for estimating what the situation may be when the dynamics of the situation may stabilize, i.e., what the basic probabilities are underlying the dynamics of the situation. The analysis is designated *Markov chain analysis,* and, if the table is in the form of the fractions of each *state of nature* (to use a jargon necessary to generalization) and ends up in some *succeeding states of nature* at the end of the time period, we have a *matrix of transitional probabilities.* Treating the information thus, we can calculate the *fixed point*—the ultimate fractional distribution among the states of nature. (An example is given below.)

There are two general forms of such Markov matrices: *absorbing chains,* and *nonabsorbing chains.* The absorbing chains deal with irreversible processes and are mainly useful in determining operating needs and standards; discussion of them is included in Chapter 8 with tools for estimating optimums. The nonabsorbing chain, however, is primarily a forecasting tool used to help us understand the forces underlying the changes that dictate the shape of the future.

Where Are We Heading? The Nonabsorbing Markov Chain. Consider our problem as members of the marketing team of Blue Sky Detergents who are evaluating the effects of our introduction of a new special duty detergent, Orion, formulated to capture parts of the market segments of two established brands, Castor and Pollux. We put Orion into test markets three months ago, with suitable promotional fanfare, and simultaneously commissioned the tabulations of a consumer purchase diary panel to be able to follow consumer buying of ours and competing products. We have met to discuss the significance of the tabulations drawn from the panel purchases in the second and third months and to see if we can divine how well we are doing. Our research analyst informs us we had 18.5 percent of the market in the third month, as compared with 43 percent for Castor and 39.5 percent for Pollux. He interprets the panel data to mean we are going to get an even larger share of the market. The tabulations, he points out, indicate that we hang onto more initial users than either Castor or Pollux do, and gain a larger share of their previous users than they get back from us.

TABLE 2-1. Brand-Switching Pattern During Third Month After Introduction of Orion Brand into the Subopolis Test Market

(Numbers indicate the fraction of the total families who purchased the brand listed to the left during the second month)

Brand bought during the second month	Brand purchased during the third month		
	Castor	Pollux	Orion
Castor	.57	.15	.28
Pollux	.15	.52	.33
Orion	.17	.16	.67

It certainly seems to us that the analyst is right, and that we have indeed a detergent whose characteristics do meet, better than either of the competing brands, the desires of a substantial segment of the market they have been getting. But we would like a more specific fix on how big that segment is. It certainly looks like better than one-fifth, but how much better? Just looking at the table as is, it is pretty hard to tell.

But suppose we look at this table as a *transitional probability matrix*, as an estimate of what the brand-switching pattern in any one month may be, at least as long as there is no change in competitor's products or in their sales promotion elements. The *first state of nature* is then the brand purchased during the second month, the *succeeding state of nature* is the brand purchased during the third month, and the *fixed point* we calculate from this matrix tells us our ultimate market share for Orion. The calculation itself is not very intricate, but, for a 3 x 3 table such as this, could involve quite a few steps. However, we can simplify the problem by not concerning ourselves with how the segments we do not snare divide up between Castor and Pollux.

We therefore revamp our tabulation into a simpler 2 x 2 table as follows:

TABLE 2-2. Simplified Brand-Switching Pattern

Purchases in second month	Purchases in third month	
	Orion	Not Orion
Orion	.67	.33
Not Orion	.30	.70

Viewed as a transition matrix, each line is viewed as the co-efficients of two variables, standing for Orion and Not Orion, and we make use of the known properties of transition probability matrices that are nonabsorbing: As the process proceeds through successive time periods, it approaches (and usually rather quickly) a limiting value we call a fixed point. This can be demonstrated empirically by trying these switching percentages out over several periods, from any starting point of quantities. At this fixed point, all lines (rows) equal each other, and all lines are identical—every figure in each vertical column is the same.

Using this knowledge, and traditional algebraic notation, the calculation of this simpler 2 x 2 table becomes:

Let: x be the Orion share
y be the Not Orion share
Then $x + y = 1$, by definition
and according to our data, $.67x + .33y = .30x + .70y$
Transposing, $.67x + .33y - .30x - .70y = 0$
$(.67x - .30x) + (.33y - .70y) = 0$
$.37x - 37y = 0$
Transposing again, $.37x = .37y$
$x = y$
Since $x + y = 1$, $2x = 1$, and $x = \frac{1}{2}$

Hence, this table of the brand switching in the third month implies that Orion will get half the market. Exactly half? Probably not. For a number of reasons, our data for the third month is not a precise estimate of the actual transition probabilities. And we probably cannot assume that the makers of Castor and Pollux are going to stand still as Orion threatens to take over a large part of their market shares. But as of now, we have a product capable of sustaining a differential advantage for perhaps between 40 percent and 60 percent of the market, and can lay out future strategy on this basis.

Note that in none of this calculation were we concerned with what the current market share was. All we needed to know was the estimate of the percentages of brand loyalty and switching, i.e., the transitional probability matrix. The Markov chain might well be dubbed the *rumor-mill model*. The final result is solely dependent on the built-in bias toward change and is unaffected by state of origin.

The nonabsorbing Markov chain would be a useful but rather specialized model to know if brand-switching problems were its only use. But it would seem a useful technique to determine the possibility of changes that might be taking place in underlying probabilities of other sorts, e.g., changes in the trend in public taste and fashion, whether they concern clothing, automobile designs, or forms of investment. Any change in basic trend would show up as a significant change in the fixed point.

Break-Even Analysis: Simulating the Estimated Relations of Price, Volume, Cost, and Profits

The effect of a planned action may be discovered by trying it out on some realistic scale in practice, or by making some very simplified assumptions about the major relationships that will determine outcome and making a number of trials, i.e., *simulations*, on paper. If our assumptions about the interrelationships are reasonable approximations, simulation is obviously the more economical course, permits the comparison of far more alternatives, and may yield as much or more unambiguous information as any real life test of feasible size. Most such simulations deal with operating level problems, but break-even analysis is really one form of simulation of wide applicability and common use worth considering in relation to price and product planning decisions. Break-even analysis is not usually thought of as a form of simulation, but a little thought will reveal that that is its true nature when used as a planning tool. Used to estimate profits under different alternatives of price and cost, this tool is one way of using highly simplified assumptions as to the relationship of price to volume, and of cost to volume.

Although the name suggests a focus on the break-even point, the main interest is probably at least as often on the behavior of profits after this point is passed. It is, of course, possible to complicate the analysis by using relatively complex assumptions as to the behavior of costs and price, but little is likely to be gained over using the simple assumption that price is stable and costs fixed over the range of output being considered (except where fixed costs are known to follow a stairstep pattern, in which case this assumption should be built into the chart). Analysis is usually in one or the other of the two forms shown in Figure 2-8 (page 50). The more conventional form shown in 2-8 A focusses attention on the fixed elements in costs, and on their recovery. Form B places the emphasis on contribution to fixed cost which can be expected at any level of output.

The method of using such charts will depend on the degree of price discretion open to management. Where management has a

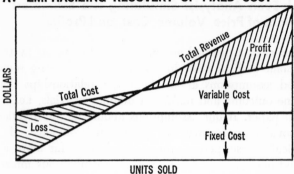

A. EMPHASIZING RECOVERY OF FIXED COST

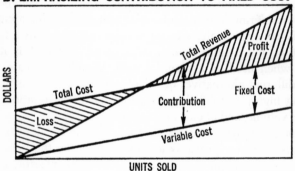

B. EMPHASIZING CONTRIBUTION TO FIXED COST

FIGURE 2-8. The Two More Common Forms of Break-Even Charts

considerable degree of latitude in quoting price, the chart can be used to estimate, under a variety of possible price alternatives, the minimum volume of sales to produce a desired profit level and the behavior of profit if volume exceeds that level. But if the market dictates a single price level, the chart can be used to indicate, for each possible alternative price structure, the minimum level of sales that must be reached to break even and the speed with which profit may be expected to rise after this level is reached. In the latter case, particularly, the emphasis is less on the break-even point itself, as the name implies, as on the behavior of the profit-volume relationship under the conditions assumed.

Price-volume relationships are usually assumed to be linear—an assumption likely to pain those with a feel for fine theoretical distinctions, and an awareness of many of the complexities of price effects. In practice, however, accurate knowledge of the exact shape of the demand curve is completely lacking and, even if known, is likely to be quite close to linear within the range of discretion open to the firm. When properly used, the revenue line is not considered as anything other than an approximation in the area adjacent to the break-even point. As with any simulation, the model used must be a simplification that focusses on the major forces and disregards minor refinements.

Construction of the break-even chart will usually be determined by the nature of the data available. If statistical or historical cost information is available which can be assumed to be reasonably valid for the intended estimate, such will be the cost information used. For all new products, and for many other situations, reliance must be placed on the analytical, or engineering, approach. The analyst examines each of the expected expenses involved and makes a judgment as to whether, over the volume range under consideration, these expenses remain constant (fixed), or vary with output, and in the latter case, how they vary, i.e., whether continuously and directly, or in some stairstep fashion. Sales revenue is usually treated as being linear, i.e., sales revenue is simply the volume expected times the unit price, and the break-even point is simply that volume at which revenue just equals total cost. Historical cost data can be adjusted for use in the case of products under production for a considerable period. The total cost line is estimated by plotting the past output-cost relationships on a scatter diagram, after adjustment for price.

One special problem involves the handling of programmed or discretionary costs, e.g., the advertising and the cost of running the personal sales operation. One way is to treat these as a separate kind of fixed cost, using only those elements specifically traceable to the particular product.

A useful variation of the break-even approach is valuable in the appraisal of elements in a product line, where the fixed costs are joint. In this case, only sales revenue and variable costs are plotted. The difference revealed is the contribution of the product to general overhead and profit at various possible volumes. This increment of revenue over and above variable cost is sometimes labelled the *profit-volume income* (*P/V* income), and is read from a chart like Figure 2-9 (below).

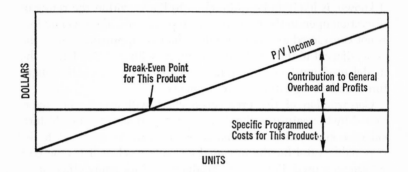

FIGURE 2-9. Profit-Volume Income Chart

The commonest type of standard for the evaluation of investments—the payout period—is really a form of break-even analysis under a different name. As in the use of break-even analysis generally, the focus of attention should be less on the pay-out period itself than on the behavior of profits after this point is passed.

Other Types of Simulation

The widespread availability of the digital computer has opened up a very wide field for both crude and more complex simulations of the results of possible alternatives, when adequate data is available. Inventory policy has been the subject of many such simulations, most commonly in one of two forms. When sufficient comparable back order experience was available, the policy has sometimes been checked against this experience. When not enough is available, it is possible to use a knowledge of the range in the number of orders, and the seasonal pattern, and to simulate the erratic receipt variability by the use of random numbers.

Markets have been simulated by programming a simplified universe composed, in its major aspects, much the same as the general market is conceived to be composed, and reacting to promotional efforts and product introduction in those ways indicated by the best available knowledge. Proposed plans could then be tested on the machine to estimate the relative outcomes.

Possible salesmen route rules can be checked against a program of the actual locations of stops, and the best of the suggested rules then fed in for the machine to lay out the route itself.

In all of these cases, the value of the simulation depends on the amount of data we have about a situation and the validity of this data in relation to the decision to be made. Simulation thus works best at the operating level where we have repetitive events unlikely to change greatly over time.

Summary

1. All business decision is in terms of specific quantities of input and expected output. He who makes the decision must interpret the figures used; to delegate the interpretation is to delegate the decision. He therefore must understand the significance of the data for the purpose used, evaluate properly the uncertainties involved, understand the simple analytical tools useful in revealing the underlying forces with which he deals, and know the capabilities and limitations of the common mathematical tools for estimating optimum values.

2. To evaluate the figures used, he must know how they were derived and how they fit the use to which they will be put; check their internal consistency and their consistency with external expectation; decide whether they are expressed in a form useful for the decision purpose; and, if they involve trends, make an estimate of the persistence of the forces making for the trend.

3. Alternatives can only be compared after discounting for their usually different degrees of uncertainty. The uncertainty estimate will be based on a combination of objective data from

past experience and subjective appraisal based on knowledge of the people and forces involved plus logical analysis from analogy.

4. Very little of the true significance of raw data is apparent without analysis. The two most useful analytical tools are the simple ones of submerging surface detail through inspection of their ordered frequency or of their chronological trends. A more tedious tool, which reveals the likely end results of a dynamic situation, is the nonabsorbing Markov chain. Simulation, which makes use of simplified knowledge of relationships, is an economical way of investigating the relative effect of many alternatives at one time.

5. Grouping data of any kind into frequency order brings out underlying consistencies not obvious from inspection of the individual figures. If we compare these ordered frequencies with the well-known normal curve, we can find out something about the existence or absence of dominant forces worth investigating. Arranged chronologically instead of by size, they can reveal unexpected trends. Comparison of two logically related frequency distributions can be very revealing as to one or both.

6. Learning curve, or process improvement, analysis is a special case of trend analysis enabling us to appraise the efficiency of task performance in which the human element enters, and suggesting that there are hidden advantages, not easily calculated, in the switch to new processes over improvement of old ones.

7. Markov chain analysis is a useful tool for determining early in the process of a dynamic change where that change is likely to stabilize, and by extension, a possible tool to reveal changes in the trend before they may be fully apparent.

8. Break-even analysis is a useful form of simulation analysis of the relation between volume and fixed costs, programmed costs, variable costs, price, and profit. The break-even point itself is sometimes a useful reference point for the evaluation of possible price, but a more important aspect is the revelation of profit behavior after the break-even point is passed.

9. The digital computer has enormously increased the scope of the cut-and-try type of simulation, permitting the testing of many operational plans against experience data.

3

Understanding and Forecasting the Demand and Supply Situation

Demand Is for a Bundle of Satisfactions

The manager's perception of the true character of the concepts of demand and supply must accord with the operational reality of these two key phenomena. His principal production and marketing decisions will be shaped by this perception. His firm exists solely to satisfy some possible market demand, and the size of that demand in a given time period is the only rational determinant of his production decisions.

Everyone, of course, knows what demand and supply are. But few indeed really understand the full behavioristic meaning of these terms, and fewer still act and forecast with a clear vision of this meaning. To the corner newsboy and the neighborhood druggist, demand is some fixed quantity of physical goods which consumers will buy from him, and the supply is also relatively fixed. The precisionist econometrician, with his graphs and formulas, recognizes that demand can vary, but still thinks in terms of homogeneous physical products in essence, ignoring the variable content of even a given physical product, as the customer views it.

The practical economic forecaster, however, soon discovers that demand is a fluid pattern of psychological relationships extremely hard to measure and even harder to forecast because of constant changes. The basic item demanded is a group of psychic services or satisfactions, not some objective physical object or service. Each service in the bundle may be furnished by any number of kinds of goods and may be only one of a number of possible services or groups of services rendered by the particular physical product offered by the firm. Demand is thus, in mathematical language, a variable—a function whose value depends on a number of factors, some controlled by management, most of them determined by customer attitudes and the culture giving rise to many of these attitudes. Forecasting requires analysis of the nature of the services that give value to the product for each of the various groups of buyers and an estimate of the factors that determine this value, and of their exact relationship to value.

Because most firms come into being to build a specific product or render a very specific service, they tend to think of this particular output as solid entities or, to use the economic expression, as homogeneous from the standpoint of the customer also. To them, the automobile buyer purchases an automobile, of a given model and type; the girl at the cosmetic counter is selecting a bottle of perfume. But however the customer may verbalize it, he does not really part with his money for a physical product or service at all. To him, the product bought is an unbreakable bundle of services, some of which he prizes highly, some of which he likes somewhat, and some of which some of the actual buyers would prefer to do without, but which they cannot separate from the other services they desire badly enough to prefer this particular bundle. The bundle valued by one customer may not be exactly the same bundle of included services his neighbor desires. Normally, there is one physical product each prefers because that particular package has, for him, a higher *net value* at the price than another at that price or some other price. The incentive that leads him to his choice is a differential value, although the price could be the same.

Consider for a moment the nature of the purchase decision in two kinds of situations.

THE CONSUMER BUYS A SUIT

The suit shopper first chooses a limited number of stores to visit—he does not visit every man's clothing department in town.

He rules out some stores because they are inconveniently located for him, and have no offsetting advantages. He thus first buys a *location service.* He automatically rules out certain stores because he considers their lines of clothes too cheap to give him the grade of tailoring he considers necessary, and others with higher-priced lines because he does not feel the extra price of the clothes is justified by the value to him of the differences in tailoring and fabric and pattern choices accounting for the higher price. He thus buys a *price-line* and *quality* group of services.

The stores he does visit are likely to be those he has found in the past to carry the kinds of clothes and the particular assortments that appeal to his taste and his pocketbook. Thus he also buys an *assortment* service within the price line. He will probably shop two or three stores at this point, because he has found all of them similar in the kinds of assortments he liked. After looking over a number of suits in these stores, he will spend some time looking at two or three models, perhaps, in one particular store. He chooses this one store finally because the items look most attractive to him. He may have found these items because the salesman was more perceptive in calling attention to the kinds of items he likes. He thus also willingly buys a *sales aid* service item in his suit.

He likes the suit finally picked because it fits well. But this latter attribute is a combination of two characteristics: (1) actual fit, in terms of size and proportioning in relation to his anatomical structure, and (2) a fit that is within limits of the current style trends as he and his reference group recognize them. His purchase thus included a *fit* and an *in-style* service. The trousers, it may be noted, actually fit much closer than he would personally prefer, but they are preferred because they meet his reference group's standards as to the correct style.

Within the range of patterns currently considered socially correct by his peers, he will pick one which appeals to his own personal taste at the moment. He will thus also have bought a *personal style* element.

Finally, he pays cash for his purchase. He probably could have charged the purchase at this store and paid the same amount of cash later. But he does not value *charge account service,* and does not wish or use it, even though he is, in some sense, paying for it.

Our consumer has, from the visible evidence, bought a suit, it is true. But what he has really purchased are store location, price lines and assortments, the style details it stocks in relation to the standards of his reference group, the pattern assortments it carries in relation to both approved styles and his personal taste, and the service of its sales personnel. The package he bought also included charge account availability he did not wish and did not use.

THE FACTORY BUYS SOME ABRASIVES

It is easy to see a differentiated product in the case of a man's suit, but what differentiation is involved in the purchasing agent's order for a supply of something as standard as industrial abrasives? What psychic returns exist other than the obvious single one of removing metal in a finishing operation? Physically, there is no discernible difference between the abrasives made by one company and those of its competitors. There is unlikely to be any difference in price. Where is the package difference which leads to a definite buying preference? For without question, a preference is there. Out of all possible suppliers, the same two are always chosen, and the purchases are meticulously divided between them in a very specific ratio: 60 percent to one supplier, 40 percent to the other. Why these two, and why two?

Consider first the choice of the one who gets the 60 percent "participation." We find he was chosen because he has well-located distributor stocks in the territory and can be depended upon to deliver on short notice in any emergency. He offers the best *availability* service. Moreover, his salesmen, and the technical representatives available to the salesman's call, have been extremely helpful in finding ways to use his different types of wheels, papers, and cloths to shorten the production process. The abrasives and their forms themselves were no different from those offered by other suppliers, but the technical representatives sent by the latter were not as useful in working out engineering details. This *engineering service* in the number one supplier's total package earned him the preferred position. But any package he could offer lacked one important element, one which only some other supplier could furnish.

The missing element which no single supplier could furnish is *insurance*—insurance against setbacks in production, which could come about because of interrupted deliveries, in case of a strike at the supplier's plant or other contingencies. So a second source had to be chosen, preferably one with nearly as good availability, at least, and good engineering service. The difference in participation granted will reflect the difference perceived in the total packages offered, up to some point. If they approach comparability, the split in purchases between the two will approach the 50-50 point.

Thus a considerable and indeed the decisive part of the abrasives product package bought was a group of intangible services developed by the sales department.

PREFERENCE-CREATING SERVICES MAY BE EITHER IN THE PHYSICAL PACKAGE, OR OUTSIDE IT

An obvious purchase of a physical product was made both in the case of the suit and in that of the abrasives order. In the case of the abrasives, the deciding preference values were completely outside the physical product; in the case of the suit, some were embodied in the suit itself (style, pattern, grade of tailoring, etc.), others were outside (store assortments, sales service). With different industrial goods, some of the differentiating services would be embodied in the physical product, as in a machine tool, for example. With other consumer products, such as lipstick, the difference might well be some outside psychological satisfaction.

Whatever the source of the difference, the buyer will pay for it in some manner if it exists for him. At times, part of the difference may be in the money price, as in the case of the suit. At times, the difference may be paid for in some other way, as in the case of the abrasives—most often by the channeling of patronage to the preferred seller, and the ruling out of other possible sources. (The latter also applied to the suit buyer in his initial choice of stores to shop.)

WHERE IS THE DEMAND ELASTICITY?

Superficially, our examples do not look like good cases for the proposition that demand is elastic. When a man sets out to shop for one suit, he is not likely to come back with two or more just because the price was a little lower than he expected. Given no change in a factory's processes, its use of abrasives is a purely fixed derived demand, entirely dependent on the rate of production.

Nevertheless, both cases conceal real elasticities, in response to the total product-price package. In rare instances, a customer might even buy a second suit if he found the price especially low, or if he found a particularly appealing fabric he had had difficulty in locating. Much more commonly, if the store service is particularly attractive, he adds some other needed purchases—belts, ties, socks, or shirts. In this way, the elasticity is in the value of sale of the store's services. He may so like the values that he increases the store's sale of suits by directing friends to it.

Nor is the derived demand of the industrial purchaser quite as fixed a ratio as it appears. If the cost and service elements in the seller's package are favorable, they may cause the buyer to make a change in process that increases the ratio of abrasives used per unit of production. The technical representative may, for example, show how the use of one particular wheel can substitute a cheaper grinding operation for a machining pass.

In either case, the quantity bought by the customer will depend on (1) the algebraic sum of the values to him, as he sees them, of the contained and attached services he desires, the price he must pay in relation to his spending power, and the amount he must set aside to satisfy desires of a higher priority, and (2) on his understanding and knowledge as to the degree and manner in which the product offered furnishes the particular bundle of services he seeks.

DEMAND IS A SET OF VALUE ATTITUDES

Demand is essentially a set of attitudes on the part of the prospective buyer. Both the desires for particular services and combinations and the acceptable manner of their satisfaction will be determined in part by physical needs and in part by the standards of the cultural subgroup to which the prospect belongs. In a fluid, dynamic society such as ours, this implies that his understanding, acceptance, and evaluation of any product is subject to constant change.

This *bundle of services* view of product carries two important implications: (1) production does not stop at the end of the assembly line, but includes the effective elements of the marketing process, the sales elements, distribution channels, and sales promotion effort and (2) individual customers will vary in their assessment of the particular portions of the bundles which have the highest value for them, and in the valuation assigned each element. The degree of preference accorded the product of any one seller is therefore an indication of the extent to which he satisfies some *particular segment* of the total market for the groups of services contained in his total product.

Both product and price are thus interdependent variables that must be managed in relation to each other if the firm is to get the kind of differential advantage that enables it to make a true profit and survive. The degree of latitude it has in the varying of either price or product will depend on the character of the physical product and the place of this physical product in the consumption pattern of the buyer. Of the two, price is easier to change and more flexible in the short run—and the more instantaneously matchable by competition. For this reason, traditional static economic theory has focussed on the pricing relationship, and the elasticity of demand relative to price, ignoring the role of product variability which renders all demand relationships dynamic.

Measurement of Demand Relationships

The concepts of *elasticity* of demand and of *cross-elasticity* of demand are the essential heart of the meaning of the economic concept of demand. The concept of elasticity is usually recognized in a vague sort of way even in popular usage of demand, when it is generally thought that a lower price can be expected to move more goods and a higher one less. The difference comes in recognizing the degrees of elasticity. The economist usually defines *elasticity of demand* as the percentage change in the quantity sold, in relation to a percentage change in the price of the product itself. *Cross-elasticity,* a closely related concept, is the recognition that the quantity of a product sold also varies with the price charged for close substitutes.

J. M. Clark has pointed out that these elasticity concepts need to be broadened, however, to include as variables the effects of sales promotion and of physical product. He also has indicated that elasticity may include changes in the margin obtained by the seller, as well as in the total revenue received.[1] This accords with the definition of product used herein, as including sales promotion. For the purposes of simplicity of discussion, let us consider these concepts in the framework of traditional price elasticity.

The crucial aspect of both concepts lies in their quantitative determination, in their possible difference in degree. The product is said to be relatively elastic when a small drop in price leads to a large increase in the quantity sold. The extreme condition makes for violent price competition. But not all types of products are highly elastic in their demand pattern. For many, a given drop in price would be matched, at best, by an equal percentage gain in units sold. Under such *unit elasticity*, the firm is no further ahead in revenue, and probably behind in total margin (if there is any substantial fixed cost in production), when it gains sales by lowering price.

For a great many products, the degree of elasticity may be far less than unity, and if management seeks increased profit, it must seek it in the direction of a product variation that will enlarge the market segments served.

In any case, price moves must take into account the degree of probable cross-elasticity with possible substitute products—products that could, under certain conditions of favorable price relationships, take over parts of the market segments now being served by the firm. The difficulties the steel industry experienced in the late 1950's, for example, stemmed directly from the industry's ignoring of the cross-elasticity of other materials in relation to some of the more important market segments for steel, especially the market for structural materials and in the container field.

Margin elasticity is a more important aspect for management

[1] John Maurice Clark, *Competition as a Dynamic Process* (Washington, D.C., The Brookings Institution, 1961), pp. 148-150.

decision than the traditional concept of price elasticity. Normally, unit margin elasticity—the price at which the total profit margin received is constant regardless of volume sold—requires a higher degree of price elasticity than mere unity. While it is rarely possible to pinpoint the degree of elasticity of any kind precisely, it is important to try to determine whether margin elasticity is greater than unity, less than unity, or about unity. Any aggressive price policy must be based on the assumption that the margin elasticity is greater than unity. Fortunately, exact measurement of the extent of the degree of this elasticity is not necessary, so long as it can be estimated whether or not it does exceed unity.

Every pricing decision makes some assumption, conscious or unconscious, about the nature of the price and margin elasticities for the product package being priced. While it is seldom possible to make an accurate estimate of the degree of elasticity, this assumption must be made consciously and carefully examined. The history of business is replete with numerous and well-known examples of failures to do just this. Perhaps the most obvious has been the failure of mass-transit utilities to examine the margin elasticities implicit in changes in fare structure, and the consequent reliance on price variation to solve the profit difficulties involved in their competition with the private auto, instead of on product variation.

QUANTITATIVE ESTIMATE OF DEMAND ELASTICITY

Any estimate of demand elasticity is bound to be an approximation, and usually a very rough one, covering a narrow range of possible variation, but this is usually enough if the relationship to unity is correct. Three general methods have been used for estimating the shape and slope of the demand curve:

1. an analysis of past prices and total demand
2. cross-sectional analysis of the market, i.e., a careful market audit, to determine who buys, what they actually seek in product service bundles, what their pattern of use, what the cost is of competing services
3. quantification of the experiences and hunches of the various sales personnel familiar with the market.

Obviously, the applicability of any of these methods varies with both product and industry, and with the availability of experienced people to make the analysis.

Time series analysis has been used largely in the field of relatively homogeneous agricultural products and other raw commodities characterized by highly competitive markets. With this sort of product and in this sort of market, price variations over time are usually variable enough and actual price quotations sufficiently in the open that some kind of meaningful analysis is possible. However, real meaning requires a time series extending over a considerable length of time, and this very time extension often means that data at the beginning of the series concern an entirely different market structure than the data at the end of the series. Development of competing substitute services and changing trends in the consumption pattern of the commodity and its place in the total consumption pattern of the user can render the whole analysis meaningless.

Thus the value of the time series approach is questionable for most manufactured goods, especially those characterized by a marked degree of product differentiation and a pattern of changing styles over time. Price *quotations* often tend to be quite stable for such products. *Actual price variation* may be quite great but tends to be concealed in the form of special concessions of one kind or another, e.g., trade-ins, ignoring of quality premiums at some periods, and rigid adherence at other periods, to mention a few. Furthermore, price is seldom the central element of competitive strategy in such situations, and its effect is difficult if not impossible to isolate from the effects of other types of competitive action.

Since it is only when a considerable degree of product differentiation is present that management has much discretion in price decision, time series analysis is weakest or even worthless in the precise areas in which management can make the most use of knowledge of price elasticity.

Cross-section analysis takes into account the buyer's alternate opportunities in the purchase decision. Management nearly always makes some use of this approach, at least to the extent of considering competing prices or the prices of substitute services when setting an initial quotation. But the executive should go beyond this to a full and detailed study of the market situation in order to pin down management's degree of discretion in the matter of price and the optimum point in its range of choice.

The price situation audit should cover at least four major points:

1. the nature of the product package perceived by the customer in the offering
2. the identity of the potential and actual customers, and how this group of prospects is segmented in terms of the service bundles they value in the physical product
3. how the needs of the prospects are being served by other products and substitutes, or how they might be so served by potential substitutes
4. the cost of use or new adoption of such possible and actual substitutes for the prospects.

The kind of information obtained from such an audit of the nature of the market being served and its alternate opportunities for satisfaction, as well as their attitudes toward the alternatives, is unlikely to yield a nicely graphable demand curve, but can go far in indicating the price opportunities facing management.

Quantification of experience simply requires bringing into the open the kinds of hunches and experience most sales managers use when making price recommendations. Even the really experienced sales executive can never outline exactly the demand curve for his product, but he usually has a pretty good hunch, which is far from being a mere guess, as to the minimum quantity he would expect to sell at a given price, and the maximum quantity he could hope to sell at this price. When he is closely questioned as to these minimums and maximums for a range of prices within the plausible extent of his past experience and observation, we can arrive at not a curve, but a zone much like that shown in Figure 3-1 (see p. 66). If we treat this zone as a case in measurement estimate, the central line in this zone would be the peak of a normal surface and thus be an estimate of the actual demand curve—one at least *as* good as the executive's experience

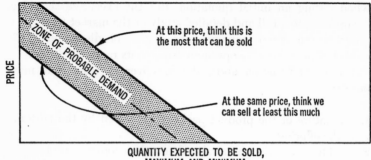

QUANTITY EXPECTED TO BE SOLD,
MAXIMUM AND MINIMUM

FIGURE 3-1. Price-Demand Relationships, Minimum and Maximum, as an Experienced Sales Executive Might Judge Them to Be

and powers of discriminatory observation. It will also be out in the open where its implications will be more visible than if he simply gives his own summary opinion as to the best price strategy without such detailed documentation.

Demand Behavior: The Kinds One Meets, and the Ways to Adapt

Product packages can be classified into about eight major groups in terms of the degree of price discretion open to management:

1. homogeneous goods
2. consumption goods with minor physical differentiation and shallow psychological or reference group influence on choice
3. products with strong psychological differentiation or marked physical differentiation
4. consumer durables
5. capital goods
6. construction services
7. raw materials and supplies sold by oligopolies in the traditional sense

8. raw materials and supplies sold by many small suppliers to a few large buyers—monopsony in the traditional static sense.

True examples of the *homogeneous goods,* with which static economic analysis occupies itself, would consist largely of consumption goods with little or no physical differentiation and no significant reference group influence or other forms of psychological differentiation, approximated by bulk staples such as sugar, salt in standard packages, and pure strain grass seed. The prices for such products is almost certain to be a market price in the static economic sense, with no discretion open to the firm for administration of the level. This is a very limited group which grows increasingly smaller.

A far more important group would be those *consumption goods* (like detergents, cigarettes, beer, gasoline) *with no significant degree of physical differentiation and very limited psychological differentiation.* Because what differentiation exists has a very low order of value to the buyer, competitors cannot permit continued price differences between closely similar product packages. (Independent cut-rate gasolines represent a different product package from that of major brand gasolines and are worth 2 cents per gallon less, in the consumer's eyes.) Competitive strategy must center on trying for sales effort elasticity by attempting to develop psychological differentiation, using intense advertising, packaging, and other methods of consumer fringe value creation and by trying for larger market segments than those served by competitors. Success is rewarded by a larger market share than competition, and the profit reward comes from greater net margin due largely to lower distribution and sales cost per unit, a form of margin elasticity of effective sales effort. It is hardly surprising that such items dominate major consumer advertising media expenditures.

Manufacture of *consumer goods with a high order of differentiation* can arise either from psychological association as with perfume or from consumer-recognized objective physical terms as with style goods. Where the differentiation is largely one of psychological association, competitive strategy would include heavy sales and advertising expenditure. It is no accident that the top percentage of sales spent for advertising in the annual tabulations of advertising expenditures (published by *Advertising Age* on the basis of tax return information), is that of the perfumes, cosmetics, and toilet preparations industry. But where the differentiation is physical, we would expect advertising expenditure to be modest, as it is, and that major efforts would be spent on design and other product development costs. In either case, we might expect frequent and durable differences in the prices of seemingly close substitutes. Price decision would largely hinge on the extent to which the seller could hope to capture other fringe market segments to which he is doing little or no selling because these fringe segments value his product difference less than does his core market segment, and on the valuation these fringe segments place on the other service elements in the package he is selling. Price elasticity in such cases is really a form of cross-elasticity between products which, in the view of some market segments, are not the same but are substitutes at a greater or lesser degree of distance from each other. Careful judgment must be exercised as to this psychological distance and the perceived value differences between the firm's own product and the service packages with which it competes.

Chevrolet's introduction of the Corvair, as its version of the compact automobile to counter the foreign-car invasion, was an interesting example of the sometimes involved nature of the comparisons buyers make and of the elements that lend value to the product differential. Partly because of the rear-engine conformation, the Corvair most closely matched the foreign sports car in consumer appeal (although not in sports car performance). Initial sales of the relatively plain introductory model were disappointing. But when a deluxe model was introduced with bucket seats at a stiff price premium, Corvair sales caught fire. The bucket seats added the missing element in the sports car image package desired by a sizeable market segment.

Many goods sold in this class must be priced to fit one of a number of traditional price lines and engineered to fit a particular price quotation. This is particularly true of garments. Price discretion is limited to determination of the line level at which the firm can best compete and of design success within the level rewarded by market share.

Consumer durable goods such as automobiles and furniture usually have a high degree of both psychological and physical differentiation. The markets tend to be highly segmented in terms of social class, regional preferences, and individual taste. The buying decision is a group one (usually the family) and is normally postponable. The ultimate flexibility of the total market is usually limited by some form of ownership goal such as two cars per family. The nature of the demand changes over the life cycle of the product, with varying proportions in at least the two main categories: (1) those segments buying the product for the first time and (2) those buying for replacement. As time goes on, the bulk of the demand becomes replacement demand, and the mode of distribution, the nature of the actual buyer (as opposed to the actual user), and the method of purchase may change radically (as in the shift in major home appliances sales from using families to contract sales to developers). The place of the product in the consumption system may change markedly also. The automobile passes from being an interesting mechanical toy, to an instrument of recreation, to a transportation necessity. The mechanical refrigerator starts out as a more convenient icebox and ends up as a major part of the food shopping and food preparation patterns.

Replacement demand may be influenced by style obsolescence or may hinge purely on physical deterioration and major advances in design that add high value services to the product. Goods highly visible to others, and which may be associated with social status, tend to style obsolescence replacement for major market segments (but seldom all segments). Thus, for many classes of people, the automobile and dress garments are more likely to be replaced by reason of style obsolescence than because of physical deterioration. Furthermore, the seller has no choice but to offer new styles if he is to maintain his market share among those market segments. On the other hand, there usually exist also some sophisticated market segments that seek to avoid buying because of frequent style changes. They choose the quiet classic designs of garments, the unchanging VW or the slowly evolving Lincoln Continental in automobiles. For the firm that knows how to design for it, this market can be very profitable, but it is a specialty market with room for few firms in any one product area.

Replacement of products not clearly visible to the neighbors, such as the washing machine, will be influenced primarily by physical deterioration and the increasing incidence of service difficulties, or by the introduction of really substantial additions to the product service bundle which acquire high value in the prospective buyer's eyes. Thus the expansion of the ice cube compartment in the home refrigerator to a freezer space of substantial capacity undoubtedly retired a lot of still operative home refrigerators of earlier design. Family finances at the moment and family expectations as to the near-future income may be a major factor in the timing of such purchases.

For nearly all consumer durables, the retail price quotation suggested by the manufacturer is simply a relatively flexible goal and should be so recognized in studying such prices. Trade-in values are commonly a very important part of the price; concessions may be made by way of tie-ins, e.g., a car radio free, or at a very reduced price, for those who buy this month; and the final sale price may even vary openly. An important part of the package bought—sometimes a major part—is the availability and quality of repair service, assumed or actual.

Capital goods such as machine tools and office equipment are normally highly differentiated from each other physically and nearly always different in associated engineering service. What is sold is primarily a system of production and the price obtainable dependent in considerable degree on the relative costs of production under the system using the particular equipment items and under some alternative system using competing equipment. Physical product is such a small part of what is commonly bought as to rate as a sales promotion in some cases. In computers, for instance, the dominance of IBM has resulted primarily from its aggressive development of "software": programming systems and assistance developed and exploited in connection with sales of their equipment.

The *construction* firm is selling its design service and experience. The bid price a firm places on its services will be judged in part on its reputation in these matters. Price strategy is not concerned with price elasticity so much as with the special technique of estimating what competing firms will bid, and their probability of getting a job for other than price reasons.

Raw materials and supplies are typically produced either by small groups of major producers approximating oligopolies in the traditional sense, or by large numbers of small suppliers selling to a few large buyers. In either case, the important determinant of demand is its derived character. The total amount bought by any customer is closely geared to his level of production. Even potentially competitive substitute materials would be adopted only after careful soul-searching about the probable duration of any advantages accruing to a changeover in production systems required by changes in materials or types of supplies. This tends to lead to sticky markets, which, once lost, are difficult or impossible to recapture. Such market stickiness can lull the firm into a complacency concerning its competitive position which can prove disastrous.

Oligopolies find it best to hold price *quotations* relatively stable and make price changes in terms of such tactics as freight concessions, forgiveness of quality premiums, and other special services. Where foresighted, they may give close attention to the use-costs of potential substitutes and exercise forbearance in price increases at times of market tightness. Where the physical product is highly standardized, as ingot copper is, for example, the competition must be in some form of customer service, or product differentiation must be achieved by integrating forward into products made from the raw materials, which can themselves be differentiated.

When the buyers are few and large and the suppliers many and relatively small, the initiative in price is in the buyer's hand, and he would tend to offer prices of whatever level would be necessary to preserve the kinds of sources of supply he needs.

Forecasting Demand Fluctuations

Good production and sales planning requires forecasts—fortunately only for the very near future with precision—of the business conditions and of their relationship to demand. The general level of demand for products whose purchase is postponable—primarily consumer durables, construction, and capital equipment—will be greatly influenced by general business conditions, as are the raw materials and supplies going into such manufacture. In addition, growth in discretionary income and in living standards can result in a sharp upward trend in the demand for many particular classes of goods. Luckily, what we know about the recent past can tell us much about what is likely to happen in the very near future, provided we have some foresight as to the general level of business in that immediately imminent period.

In the case of some products, the demand lags behind changes in the business level sufficiently so that we merely need the available figures on the recent level to predict changes in the demand. Changes in the level of production of castings, for example, lag changes in the rate of increase or decrease of general business by just about six months. Some similar relationship would be true of many raw materials and supplies.

Some other means of forecasting must be found for products like machine tools whose ordering tends to signal a change in general economic conditions. In general, for such items we must find out what those who will be doing the ordering plan to do. Since plans must be made in advance, such information is usually available and is reasonably useful, although plans are always subject to change.

Mere study of lead-lag relationships to national income and production estimates are not in themselves enough for safe prediction in many industries. Other kinds of information of specific relevance to the individual industry must be analyzed. Automobile industry economists, for example, pay close attention to the extent of the change in consumer instalment debt. A decrease in total consumer debt foretells of an increase in the amount of spending power available for automobile purchases, and conversely, an increase in the debt level foretells a period of harder selling. Changes in the age composition of the population can have considerable effect on the purchase of automobiles and of many other kinds of goods. A relatively narrow age range buys a disproportionately large proportion of the new cars (thirty-five to forty-five).

Makers of appliances are particularly interested in the changes in proportions of those of marriageable age and in the trends in actual family formation. Most appliances are bought either directly or indirectly by those in the early years of their married life. By good fortune, most such relationships that are important to sellers are stable elements in the culture pattern. What has happened in the past can be expected to happen in much the same way in the future.

Many classes of product, especially the expendable consumer items with a relatively inelastic demand are, of course, relatively unaffected by economic conditions.

Management of Supply

The supply situation is more likely to be taken for granted than is demand. Nevertheless, long-run profits can be greatly affected by the way supply itself is managed. Supply is variable, and although adjustments seldom respond immediately to stimulating or depressing incentives, respond they do to actions a big buyer takes.

As a buyer of parts, raw materials, supplies, and of labor, the business man buys a package of services just as any other buyer does. He is on one side of a demand curve that is no different than when viewed from the seller's side. Effects of too-close bargaining are usually delayed, but labor, materials, and supplies are price-elastic. One of the reasons for shortages of really skilled secretaries and of really skilled, experienced engineers in the last decade has been the vanishing premium paid for real skill and experience over and above the pay any relatively unskilled beginner could demand and get.

The industrial buyer is commonly thought, correctly, to be a relatively rational buyer, but he does sometimes set up specifications for some items that include services of no objective value to him. He may thus by-pass service packages containing elements he over-discounts, even those that may have no effect on the utility of the item for his purposes. A smart buyer can often find potential supplies in the market which have more value to him than the traditional ones—supplies being by-passed by other buyers because of supposed defects. Those, for instance, who hire workers of a type being discriminated against, e.g., the handicapped, minority groups, older workers, often reap disproportionately large productivity benefits. Bargains are found by perceiving valuable services in a product which are being ignored by the bulk of the market. Artificial specifications that do not add real value to whatever is bought and specifications incompatible with the basic performance values sought are a frequent source of lost profit.

The key to supply management is careful conscious attention to the kind of service performances really needed from a purchase and a careful evaluation of the worth of each service in the overall production system. The relative novelty, as yet, of value analysis and the spectacular gains often resulting from its adoption are clear testimony that industry often loses sight of the basic performance desired in designing and in purchasing. Extension of the value analysis approach to hiring could often achieve even more dramatic consequences. One executive in charge of a large statistical and stenographic staff of women was plagued with heavy turnover and careless work until, in desperation, he reversed the age specifications in use and decreed that only women *over* 35 be hired. As he noted later, "There isn't quite so much glamor around our office now, but, boy, we sure get out the work!" If the positions available advertisements are any index, many companies are putting a similar stress on youth for staff positions where experience is a prime value.

Summary

1. Market demand is not some fixed quantity of a physical product which can be sold, but a fluid and changing value which prospective buyers put on the bundles of psychological services they expect to obtain from the offerings of the seller. The bundle desired will vary from one prospect to another, as will the values placed on the constituent services in a given physical offering from one individual buyer to another. This implies that any one physical product is usually several different products in the sense that it may serve several quite distinct market segments, and also that demand can be satisfied by quite different physical products.

2. Some of the services demanded may be inherent in the physical product. Quite usually, a considerable number of the values the customer sees in the product come from outside the physical

item sold and are furnished by the advertising and personal sales operation and by the distribution channels.

3. All economic concepts of demand center on the twin constructs of *elasticity* and *cross-elasticity* of demand, stated precisely as the percentage change in the quantity sold related to the percentage change in price of the product (ordinary elasticity) and of competing substitutes (cross-elasticity) respectively, in the form used in traditional static economics. When dealing with the dynamics of the market we must recognize other comparable forms of elasticity: sales promotion elasticity, product variation elasticity, and profit margin elasticity.

4. The estimate of elasticity present must be an approximation at best. Luckily, business decision usually hinges on little more than the relationship of the elasticity faced to unity. Of the three methods of estimate, *time series analysis* of past prices and total demand is of little use in those markets characterized by product differentiation. *Cross-section audits* of what services the customer is buying and of competing services can be very helpful in making a decision but do not usually yield a nice precise set of demand curves. *Quantification of the hunches and experience* of sales executives can give something resembling a demand curve, but only within the range of knowledge of those queried, and with only the precision of their powers of observation.

5. Demand behavior, and management's latitude of discretion in stimulating it by varying price, varies greatly between different kinds of product packages. Only those packages that are strongly differentiated from the closest substitutes leave management much discretion in choosing the price quotation. Eight different kinds of product packages can be found: homogeneous goods, consumption goods whose differentiation is of minor value to the buyer, consumer durables, capital goods, construction services, raw materials and supplies sold by oligopolies in the traditional sense, and raw materials and supplies sold by many small suppliers to a few large buyers. Each has its own kind of demand characteristics to which decision must be adapted.

6. For products other than consumer expendables with relatively inelastic demand, the fluctuation of demand with general business conditions must usually be taken into account in the

preparation of production and sales plans. Fortunately, the crucial part of the demand forecast is that for the proximate future, and we can do a fairly good job of forecasting the very near future on the basis of what is known about the present. In some cases, little more needs to be known than the relationship of changes in demand for a class of product to changes in the trend of business. More usually, factors other than the lead-lag relationships need to be known, e.g., factors peculiarly affecting the demand for a particular industry's products, such as population changes, debt levels, marriage rates, and others.

7. Supply also needs to be managed. As a buyer, business has more discretion in the price offered than it usually does for those it charges, and it must shape its offering to maintain or improve the available supply of labor, material, and operating supplies needed. In addition, profit is to be had from a careful consideration of the kinds of services really needed in what it purchases, to the end that specifications do not require characteristics costing more than they are worth to the buyer, or even that the main emphasis is not put on specifications incompatible with the main values desired in production.

4

Competition: Management of the Product Variable

THE CONCEPT of competition is probably surrounded by more confusion, even among economists themselves, than any other concept of economics. A cultural schizophrenia as to its necessity for the public welfare is probably one reason. As customers, we all desire the most rigorous competition among our suppliers, and we have a number of very important laws whose intent, at least, is to insure that they do compete. On the other hand, it has been aptly noted that "competition is the life of trade but the death of a business"—that rigorous head-on competition can wound deeply when practiced. So, when we are not doing the buying, we are likely to feel that competition ought to be "fair," that it ought to be kept within some kind of gentlemanly rules, like tennis. The result is considerable confusion as to the effect of pricing decisions, and as to the true source of profit.

The really fundamental confusion, however, results from an enormous blind spot as to the full contents of the product package the customer desires and pays for, and from a total disregard of the observable fact that this product package is and must be the principal variable of competitive strategy. Traditional static economics, and legal minds and the public in general, have assumed away this conspicuous fact of life and focussed on price quotations as the central fact of competition. Product has been thought of as some solid, physical object or contract which is, in the economist's jargon, "homogeneous," i.e., practically identical as between competing firms. And as the term *administrated prices* indicates, the modern large industrial firm has been thought to have a great deal of discretion in pricing. Even some thirty years after the publication of Chamberlain's historic analysis of monopolistic competition, most economic texts treat of product differentiation, if at all, as a minor case not worthy of extended treatment. Yet as J. M. Clark, in his long overdue treatment of *Competition as a Dynamic Process*[1] has pointed out, product differentiation is the general case, and anything else an exception, in the actual business world, and inevitably so in a dynamic society.

Clark has emphasized the seemingly obvious point that competition really involves four variables as he has defined them: price, physical product design, selling effort, and cost. He has supported his analysis with both thorough theoretical care, and with reference to everyday experience and observation. For purposes of management decision, however, the author prefers to return to the simpler traditional dichotomy of price and product, defining both as the customer views them, i.e., *price* as all sacrifices, *product* as a total bundle of valued psychological satisfactions. Of these two sides of competition, the seller has wide latitude in the product package, often very little in price. The basic element of strategy must then be product.

Product Is Whatever the Customer Pays For

The only realistic definition of product is *value*. Product consists of all elements in the producer's offering, and in the total sales situation, for which some group of customers will pay a price. Put another way, product is customer-perceived desired performances. This definition has two critical corollaries: (1) If the customer sees a benefit, it is there, and if he does not, it does not exist and (2) The physical form of the product does not in any sense define the competition.

Two items completely different in their physical form, or even resulting in obviously different physical types of performance,

[1] J. M. Clark, *Competition as a Dynamic Process* (Washington, D.C., The Brookings Institution, 1961).

may yet fulfill identical satisfaction needs of the customer. The automatic washing machine and the centralized laundry may be, for a given group of potential customers, in direct competition. The hog raiser may choose between antibiotic feed additives and stricter sanitation practices. Two products are competitive if a substantial segment of the potential market considers one as an adequate substitute for the other, at the prices available. Note that this erases the common distinction sometimes made between competing products and substitute products, because the customer makes no such distinction.

Customers are even less homogeneous than products. The psychological satisfactions desired, and the relative priority of value placed on them, will vary from one customer to the next. Each will want a somewhat different total package than the next and willingly pay a different price for the varied elements in that package. But the economics of industrial production require that the number of competing differentiations be rather limited. Thus the customer normally buys a compromise, a package that comes closest to what he really wants, but which may omit some things he would like, and may include some service elements he considers of no value.

A *market segment* thus becomes a substantial group of customers giving preference to a given satisfaction bundle that matches no individual's desires exactly, but which has a total value to each greater than any other bundle he considers as competing. The "consumer's surplus" of traditional economic price theory arises because the seller's price must be the lowest common denominator of the satisfaction values of the market segment he desires to cover. Since most buyers' satisfactions are never precisely fulfilled, potential competition always has the opportunity to develop a different satisfaction package that will come closer to the desires of some portion of this segment and some portions of other producers' segments, at a price attractive to the newly defined segment.

The physical product is not only just a part of the total package, and at times a very minor part; there are occasions when it may simply be an element of sales promotion for the nonphysical package—the real item purchased. In one sense, the industrial abrasives purchase example was a case in point. The total list of benefits for which the customer will pay in some manner include:

1. received physical performance rendered by the physical aspects of product
2. perceived social benefits represented by the consumption, use, or even mere possession of the product
3. psychological benefits rendered by the mental association of the product with otherwise irrelevant attributes (social status with the Cadillac, romance with the Chanel No. 5 perfume, etc.)
4. objective benefits conferred by the location, manner, and timing of purchase availability
5. subjective benefits conferred by the location in which purchased and the time and manner of the transaction (worth more if bought at Neiman-Marcus than if purchased from Woolworth's)
6. instructional, informational, and technical services furnished by the seller in promoting the sale of the product (the engineering help furnished by the abrasives manufacturer)
7. the assurance of dependability and quality rendered by the knowledge of brand or source
8. an assortment benefit—the availability of a wide line to choose from or the availability of a large number of different kinds of items from a single dependable source (reducing the costs of transaction).

Only physical performance is inherent in the product itself, and then only to the extent that the buyer perceives it. The perception of the benefit may well originate outside the product from the customs and mores of the group. In their first year in Utah, the Mormons saw only the threat of disaster to their food crop—wheat—in the invasion of crickets, and erected a statue to the gulls whose intervention saved the wheat. But the nearby Indians would have reversed the roles. To them the crickets would have been a heaven-sent feast, the gulls a menace to their food supply.

Whatever the source of the perception and whatever the benefit perceived, whether it be physical performance, social prestige, or merely personal enjoyment, the fact that the customer will add to the price to get it is both necessary and sufficient evidence that he gets something he desires in return, something not available in "competing" products. His perception of the taste qualities, which lead him to pay a premium for a fine vintage wine, for example, are as much a part of the product as the chemistry of that wine. And this perception is as much a part of the production process as the fermentation and bottling, whether the perception comes from knowledge acquired by growing up in a wine-conscious culture or is the result of the publicity, advertising, and educational efforts of the Wine Institute.

Production Cost Includes the Cost of Selling

Since some of the satisfactions the customer willingly pays for result from the sales effort, selling is part of production, and its cost part of the production cost. If production takes place only when and if the customer will pay for the result, then any selling effort is an integral part of production if the customer will pay more as a result of it. (Actually, of course, it is hard to conceive of many situations in which any purchases come about without some selling efforts—at least the minimum of advertising necessary to inform the customer of the availability of a desired item.)

Indeed, the substitution of selling for production effort, and the reverse, can often be seen. One manufacturer of standard industrial fasteners (nuts, bolts, rivets, etc.), for example, built a multi-million dollar annual volume by substituting the extra production expenses of short runs and rush production for the selling forces used by others. He used no salesmen, seldom did any personal contact work on his own, and incurred no other sales expenses except a monthly letter listing sizes available for immediate shipment, interlarded with some cleverly written comments and amusing items. He sold the same accounts his bigger competitors also depended upon. But he went far beyond any competitor in willingness to make quick deliveries on short notice. He even kept a business telephone extension by his bedside and would accept calls in the middle of the night from any customer in need of an emergency shipment. If such an occasion arose, he would go immediately to the plant, stop other production if necessary to get the order out, and have it moving by air express by morning.

Obviously such tactics raised the costs of his physical production. But his sales costs were lower, and he got a profitable share of the market.

Substitutibility Is the Measure of Competition

Two products, whatever their individual physical forms, are in competition to the degree the customer is willing to accept one as a substitute for the other without discount or premium in cost or share of his purchases. *Only when he is completely indifferent, either in terms of price willingly paid, or in the proportion of his trade, can products be considered fully competitive.* Otherwise, he perceives some differentiation in the total package available.

Differentiation is primarily a matter of consumer perception and belief, and only incidentally, if at all, a matter of physical design. If the customer will pay more for a can of peaches with the Del Monte label than for some other can with a less well-known brand name packed from the same crop, to the same grade, by the same standards, in the same factory (as well he might), he does so because he believes the two to be different (perhaps in dependability of quality) even when he is aware that they originate at the same cannery. If he pays 2 cents more for gasoline from a Standard or Texaco pump than for gasoline bought from a local independent, which comes out of the same refinery blending tanks, and which he knows gives the same mileage, he does so because he perceives a 2 cents per gallon difference in the total station and service packages offered. And if the physician prescribes Aureomycin rather than the same tetracycline drug under its generic name, it is because he feels there may be a difference in quality even though he knows both must meet the strict standards of the FDA.

From the economic point of view, whatever produces such differences in perception and belief must be viewed as production processes and the customer's reluctance to substitute must be viewed as an indication of incomplete competition.

A Practical Model of the Competitive Process

Any decision as to business strategy and tactics is a decision as to how to meet competition and thus must be based on a correct picture of the way competition actually operates in the marketplace. This picture, or *model*, is, in turn, completely determined by the assumptions made as to the nature of product, as defined by the dynamics of that marketplace. Hence the emphasis placed on the right definition in the foregoing discussion.

There are essentially three possible models of the competitive process, each, of course, with some minor variations:

1. the model of traditional static price economics, which focusses exclusively on price as the mechanism of competition, and analyzes phenomena in terms of pure competition, pure monopoly, and impure or imperfect competition
2. the popular or moralistic concept of competition, which also focusses primarily on price and seeks standards of "fair price," "fair trade," and "acceptable" competitive price tactics
3. the model of monopolistic competition (in Clark's terms, effective competition), which recognizes that competition is a dynamic process, that the source of true profit must be innovation in such a dynamic situation, and that this inevitably leads to product competition as the primary basis of competitive strategy, with price primarily useful in the carrying out of short-run tactical objectives.

The price economics of the traditional textbook has sought mathematical precision by assuming away any possibility of progress or dynamics, because recognition of the importance of innovation destroys the possibility of equilibrium solutions. The same precisionist desire has led economists to define product as "homogeneous" as between competitors. While we can all sympathize with any desire for more definitive and precise solutions, the fact of life is that these two assumptions remove us completely from the realities of any known market. More important, they lead business decision and political attention away from a focus on the true source of profit and of economic progress which is constant innovation and thus universal differentiation of product. Indeed, although few economists consider that they have much in common with the advocates of the soft competition of *fair trade* (price maintenance), these latter are simply following a warped corollary of the postulates of traditional static economics. Discussion of the reasoning of this moralistic school is best left to the discussion of price tactics.

By contrast, the model of monopolistic, or effective, competition is based on a frank recognition of the wide heterogeneity of customers, their needs and desires, and the widely varying values placed on the satisfaction of any given desire. This consumer-oriented model perceives that, in such a diverse market, product cannot remain homogeneous, since the way to profit is to satisfy the needs of some large segment better than they are currently being met—at the expense of doing as good a job for some other segment. It also forsakes any hope of achieving precise equilibrium solutions, since what one man develops as an innovation, another can soon copy or, if he is wise, improve upon. All adjustments are therefore temporary and approximate.

Given these realistic assumptions, we would expect no two successful sellers to be offering identical products as viewed by the customer. We would find that physical product would not necessarily define competition, but that a considerable part of the competition a manufacturer would meet would cross the boundaries of physical product classes. We would find little in common between the cost structures of individual manufacturers and "industry," a fuzzy concept which defined competition for only one aspect of a seller's product. Competition, we would have to conclude, is partial and a chain phenomenon—what J. M. Clark has very aptly called "chain oligopoly." That is, each seller is in competition with a limited group of other sellers with regard to some of the aspects of his product, and with different sellers for different aspects. These other sellers, in turn, are in competition with others with respect to product attributes not included in the product of the first seller, and so on.

One way to comprehend this picture of competition is to picture it in terms suggested by an early designation—"valley monopoly." If we turn this around to a more realistic assessment of *mountain peak monopoly—valley oligopoly,* we can depict such a system graphically, in three-dimensional form.

MONOPOLISTIC COMPETITION: A HIGHLY SIMPLIFIED GRAPHIC ANALOGY

We can attempt to visualize the essence of this view of competition with the aid of a simplified graph such as Figure 4-1. As depicted here, the three products, **A, B,** and **C,** compete directly for that market segment interested in the core satisfaction-

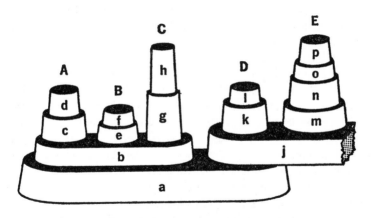

Capital letters A, B, C, D and E represent products, each having four satisfaction-attributes labelled by the lower case letters a through p.
(Note that A, B, and C share attributes a and b. D shares a only with these other 3 products, but shares j with product E.)

Vertical distances represent the value perceived in the attribute by a market subsegment whose size is represented by the horizontal dimension of the plateau outlined and labelled by the attribute.

FIGURE 4-1. Highly Simplified Graph Analogy of the Typical Competitive Chain-Oligopoly Situation

attributes **a** and **b,** and if the price is not above the level of the two, that fringe part of the market segment in the valleys between the peaks will shift freely between the three. But those subsegments that value any of the satisfaction attributes **c, d, e, f, g,** or **h** will purchase only the individual product containing the element valued. For that market segment seeing value in **a,** but not **b,** a fringe portion also sees product **D** as an alternate choice, putting **D** in competition with **A, B,** and **C** for this segment, if the cost is no higher than the value perceived in **a.** In turn, **D** has some different satisfaction attributes: **j, k,** and **l.** One attribute, **j,** is shared with product **E** and some others not shown that have no satisfaction-package elements in common with **A, B,** or **C.** Thus, **D** is in competition with **A, B,** and **C** for part of its market, and with **E** and some others not shown for some other parts. But **E** is not in competition with either **A, B,** or **C,** since customers perceive no satisfaction elements in common between **E** and these others. **D** also has some loyal customers who wish the attributes **k** and **l** and will purchase nothing but **D** so long as the price is not above the value level of the top of **l.** For this small subsegment of a market, **D** is a monopolist. Where he prices will depend on whether it is more profitable to confine himself to serving the subsegment interested in all four attributes or to raid some of the much larger segment which sees no value in any characteristics beyond **a** if he desires part of the market held by **A, B,** or **C,** or, alternately, that segment interested only in the service of **j** if he wishes to raid the market share of **E** and some others.

This graph also indicates one very important source of price elasticity: the existence of different market segments which value different elements at different levels in the satisfaction package. If we refer back to the graph, we can see one product with little choice to aim for anything but the general market—product **B.** The value level of its differentiating characteristics is too low to be worth much. Product **C,** on the other hand, has differentiating characteristics appealing to a very narrow market subsegment, but is assigned a very high value by this narrow segment. It might well be profitable to charge what this narrow segment willingly pays and make no attempt to get any of the fringe in the valley.

This graphic analogy is, of course, highly oversimplified. Only two links of a chain are shown, whereas, in reality, the situation will chain out in every direction, and few competitors are likely to have more than a single differentiating characteristic. Indeed, quite often, the only differentiation is likely to be in the particular combination of attributes shared by other firms and in the proportioning of them. But this analogy should render more visible some of the strong incentives to constant change in the competitive situation, incentives that have made product differentiation a relatively universal *must* of the business scene. Even in the sale of farm products, anything approaching pure competition is disappearing with the growth of the industrialized farm. Even in that most widespread of farm production activities, e.g., egg production, the market structure is now approaching the point where producers without an established marketing organization and outlet may be unable to sell or must take ruinous discounts. There is strong market preference in the channels of trade, i.e., differentiation.

DIFFERENTIATION IS INESCAPABLE

A corollary of this concept of market competition is that, in an economy of abundance, a firm *must* differentiate, and also that differentiation will occur whether or not it is an aim. The seller must give the customer a reason to prefer his particular offering. Two firms with seemingly completely substitutable products cannot continue to compete on equal footing. One or the other will sooner or later lose out due to accidental differentiation. Customers come to think of one as a more dependable source of supply, or dealers find his products moving off the shelves faster and drop the other. If the physical product is one requiring some degree of after-purchase technical service, the mere fact of a market share loss can feed back into snowballing consumer loss of preference. Witness the speed with which declining automobile makes disappeared once share of market started a decline.

Conversely, it is obviously futile to attempt to simply duplicate the product strategy and price of an established competitor. The fact that his market segment knows what to expect from him, and not from the newcomer, becomes a differentiating element in itself—one which a duplicate product gives the customer no reason to investigate. In addition, with nothing better to offer the customer, distributors will not make room on their shelves for such an item.

One interesting sidelight of this concept is that if substitutability, as seen by the customer, is quite high, we would expect sellers to attempt to capture their markets by outright purchase. This is, in fact, what happens when buyers cannot find a difference in the product. Ingot copper, for example, is identical whether you buy it from Anaconda, Kennecott, or American Smelting and Refining. Its shape is the same and its purity is identical (99.99 percent copper). As a result, every important producer has developed or purchased major fabricating facilities that turn out alloy materials and wire with some degree of differentiation.

SUCCESSFUL PRODUCT PLANNING SEES THE PRODUCT THROUGH THE CUSTOMER'S EYES

Since product is value, product planning must be planning to give the customer added value, as the customer would perceive that value. Such product planning must start with accurate knowledge of what the company is selling, and what more it could sell, that would have value to the buyer. There must be a clear understanding of the benefit elements in the packages being produced and in those proposed, i.e., those elements in which the seller has or can create a temporary monopoly preference. A market innovation is not just something new and different; it is a new service element the customer is psychologically prepared to find attractive, when properly presented and dramatized.

The automobile industry has presented some of the more visible cases of not uncommon business disasters resulting from a lack of comprehension of what the seller was actually being paid for, and of the effect of projected product plans on the benefit packages being offered. For many years, the prestige name in luxury automobiles was Packard. The prestige, and eventually the enterprise itself, was extinguished when the company tried to couple its luxury models with a moderately-priced line under the same name, the Packard Clipper. The Clipper's advent destroyed the aura of exclusiveness and social status comprising the major part of the value being bought. Studebaker got a jump on the post-World War II automobile market with a clean-lined compact design that set the pace of body design for the other makes. But the company was so completely unaware of what gave sales such a break-through push that it went into a different design trend and used a mistaken promotion, thus alienating the very market segments it had attracted, and drowned its domestic operation in red ink. The much bigger and stronger Chrysler Corporation has, thrice in its history, so thoroughly mistaken the merely different with true market innovation that it came very close to the same disaster: with the 1934 Airflow Desoto, again in 1950 with the entire line, and finally in 1962 with the "long, lean look" in the Dodge and Plymouth lines.

Furthermore, the desires, for the fulfillment of which the customer will pay, change in value and in kind. The company must be alert to those elements in its satisfaction package which are or which become unattractive for a large part of the segment who nevertheless have continued to buy because of the valued elements. Otherwise, competitors can, and eventually will, nibble off portions of the firm's market segment, as they did to Henry Ford in the 1920's, copying his mass-production appeal with elements of style and convenience, and adding breadth of choice the elder Ford refused to deliver. Without question, one of the best areas in which to seek innovation opportunities is in the irritations of customers with present products—particularly your own.

All innovation, of course, is not in the physical design of the product. Mere discovery of valuable unrealized uses for a product and their vigorous promotion creates just as much new consumer benefit as though a new product had been developed. From the customer's viewpoint, there is no difference. Successful creation of the association of glamor and beauty with a new lipstick color is just as much a consumer benefit as though some magic hypnosis had created greater confidence and poise in the young purchaser. The result is the same.

We cannot argue with the customer's perception, beyond objective matters such as those of technical performance, health, and nutrition. If he thinks a benefit is there and has a given value, it *is* there, in the only place that counts, in his satisfaction. Physicians have long known that the physically inactive placebo can truly relieve pain in a certain segment of the populace, and the relief is no different from that furnished by a really effective analgesic.

Optimizing Product Development

The product difference is the only reason the customer buys from you rather than from someone else. But the product difference is ephemeral. What you have accomplished, someone else not only can, but will, duplicate and improve upon. Innovation—product development in its broadest sense—must be constant. This product planning must be directed in the light of the answer to two fundamental questions:

1. What opportunities for new customer services can be divined from the developing pattern of the economy, the technology, or the culture; from the stresses that develop in our business experience; or from customer dissatisfaction, irritations, and inconveniences?
2. Which of these opportunities are for us—which ones take the kinds of knowledge and skills in which we excel and are within our resources to exploit?

Historically, of course, much innovation has been the result of lucky coincidence between the innovator's personal wishes and tastes and those of the market. Such was probably the basis of Henry Ford's early success. But even in the past, most great enterprises originated from the sharp personal observation and analytical imagination of those who built them, from simple crude observation of market developments, of customer attitudes and problems, and of customer use systems. Very little has come directly out of research, and the latter will probably continue to play a supporting role.

Nevertheless, when directed with insight and imagination, skilled research analysis can often do much to uncover profit opportunities. One dramatic example was the development of the sculptured velvet rug in the 1940's. Researchers testing for market acceptance of rug designs discovered that consumers preferred the texture of the ordinary velvet rug to that of other weaves but were quite unhappy with the track marks such rugs plainly showed. When this was pointed out, weavers developed the twist loop rug, to obviate track marks, but it lacked the desired texture. Although it did succeed, analysts found customers still would like a trackless true velvet. At their insistence, designers of one company tried various approaches, finally hitting on the sculptured weave. It was an immediate success and, like most good ideas, easy to reproduce and was soon copied by all manufacturers.

Although the end result was a different physical product, note that what research insight created was simply an idea—one that the product finally embodied. The substance of innovation is the idea, not the product.

INNOVATION IS MUCH MORE THAN PHYSICAL INVENTION

The "new product" may simply be the result of publishing or dramatizing hitherto unrecognized services or potential services, from the reproportioning of different elements in the total product, merely from improved quality control, or from sales arrangements that simplify the customer's business or personal planning, for example.

Breweries had long been using steam cleaning on returned bottles, but Schlitz achieved its first break-through to national preference by telling the public about it and dramatizing its interest in sanitation. This advertising insight made Schlitz a "new" product, i.e., differentiated it.

A different kind of imaginative advertising built a "new product" out of a camouflage cosmetic which had not been able to maintain enough volume to stay in the stores. The originator developed it to cover a disfiguring facial birthmark and promoted it purely for this purpose. After its initial lack of success in developing volume, two imaginative promoters picked it up and had insight enough to push it to cover minor facial blemishes, advertising and selling via a direct sales TV program featuring comparisons of movie stars with and without makeup, and coupling the advertising with sound makeup advice. The result was a sustained sales volume which put it back to stay on department store cosmetic counters.

As already pointed out, an important part of the product sold in industrial marketing is the accompanying technical service. Different customer segments, however, may wish different amounts of this service, and some may actively desire its complete omission. If this segment is large enough, there is an opportunity for a seller of a "stripped" product at a stripped price. Something of this sort seems to have been the occasion for the heavy downward pressure of recent years on the price of polyvinyl chloride resin. As with all really new materials, when PVC first came on the market, producers had to develop sales through free technical assistance in production methods and proper design for this plastic. As time went on, the larger users developed their own expertise in its use, and even their own confidential know-how. Many had know-how they preferred not to share and wanted no part of outside technical personnel around their operations. They became ready customers of new producers who set up streamlined operations, selling only the basic types of resin and selling without technical representatives and with the minimum of sales organization, often just a telephone and a price list.

Uniformity of quality, at a reasonably acceptable level, is often the attribute most desired in a manufacturing raw material and in many consumer goods. This has been one of the great attractions of synthetic materials competing directly with natural raw materials. (Another attraction has been the possibility of stable cost.) Because of the extreme variability of size and quality of the natural crystalline mineral, mica, for example, large users have spent several times its annual cost trying to find synthetic substitutes giving somewhere near the unique dielectric values that make it a key item in much electrical manufacturing. The variable cost of using the natural material is so wide, even when the unit price is stable, as to make nonsense out of any attempt to cost-account the fabricating process of making mica parts.

Many other forms of differentiation could be mentioned which are independent of the physical product itself, among them, widespread availability of distribution, time of delivery, psychological associations developed by imaginative advertising, publicity, or even accidentally, the furnishing of credit, or guarantee of continuance of future supply at some minimum level.

Source and dependability of supply, for example, is the only distinguishing difference between "primary" and "secondary" aluminum alloy ingot. Buyers are quite aware that they are identical in composition and both made of mixtures of secondary and primary metal. Secondary ingot is so designated because it is produced by firms that do not refine primary metal themselves. When total aluminum supply is plentiful, the secondary sells at a heavy discount relative to the price of the primary alloy ingots. Buyers avoid secondary at such times because they wish to establish a historical usage base with the primary refiners in anticipation of the recurrent periods of short supply incident to the growth of aluminum use and production. The primary is thus worth more in times of easy supply because it carries with it a ration ticket for use in times of shortage (when the unrationed secondary may sell for more than the primary).

In sum, product differentiation, which causes the customer to prefer one firm's offering over a close or even physically identical substitute, need not be in physical form, and a product can be an innovation without the aid of physical invention.

SOURCES OF POTENTIAL PRODUCT INNOVATION

Since product is consumer value, product innovation consists of adding substantially to the values now available to the buyer. Valuable new product ideas can be obtained in one of four ways:

1. looking for product ideas needed to complete whole new technologies already in demand, but held back by lack of a key component (When developed, such innovations offer the greatest added value.)
2. looking at the needs of a future that is inherent in the present
3. searching for weaknesses in the firm's ability to serve the customer, e.g., product attributes that make the company vulnerable to competitive products, keep its costs high, or seem to

endanger the business in other ways, and converting these problems into opportunities

4. studying the customer and his product use directly, i.e., finding out his irritations and unsatisfied needs, studying his consumption systems with regard to the products he uses, and analyzing the trends in his tastes and attitudes.

Finding Missing Components for New Technological Systems. The development of service elements that make available a complete new technological system for which the customer is ready offers the greatest advance in consumer value and the most potential profit to the firm. Such innovations gain tremendous leverage from the other elements that are ready to fall into place, and their discovery and development is more a matter of insight than engineering.

The farm tractor has been around in some form at least as long as the automobile. But the tractor did not drive the horse and mule from the field until long after they had vanished from the highway. The doom of the Belgians and Percherons came with the development of a very simple physical invention in the 1930's: the rubber tractor tire, giving the tractor a footing which did not pack the soil and permitted over-the-road speeds.

In computers, according to the reporters for *Fortune,* it is now "Fortress" IBM. But IBM neither invented the computer nor introduced the first models to the market. What IBM developed was the *software* which made the computer technology available to any medium or large office without the services of scarce mathematicians. IBM aggressively developed and promoted the needed nonphysical service of program libraries, simplified programming languages and programming programs, and intensive educational and engineering service.

Products for the Future That Is Here. Another excellent source of ideas for new consumer values is the anticipation of the needs of a future whose shape will inevitably be quite different from the shape of today. Fortunately, not all of that future is hidden in the cloudy recesses of a crystal ball. Some of it is as clearly visible in the facts of the present as the hay harvest is in the first green sprouts of spring grass, and for much the same reason.

Much of the future will be a natural maturation of visible forces already set in motion. Peter Drucker [2] has indicated four kinds of changes that will give rise to new product opportunities:

1. population changes in size, composition, residence, and other characteristics
2. new knowledge, both in the industry and in the general fund of knowledge which could affect the business
3. changes in industry and market structure
4. changes in other countries or markets likely to foretell of similar changes in the firm's own market.

Few would contend that the *population* tabulations make for exciting reading, but the firms who can read into them the inherent trends they contain will be tomorrow's leading competitors. They will be the firms who see the opportunities for new volume needs because of the developing of new market segments. The size and nature of many fundamental needs and desires of tomorrow's markets can be read from trends revealed by those drab columns of figures in the Census. It was Robert Wood's recognition of such Census trends which led Sears to seek aggressive expansion in the large cities of the country and put it far ahead of the competing mail-order houses long before other firms discovered the strong trend to urban living.

We need only to know the age and sex distribution of today's population to learn what the different age and sex distribution will be ten and twenty years hence and to infer which of the population segments now relatively unimportant will become important population segments and market segments with special needs of a foreseeable type, worth cultivating. Looking at the recent trends in occupations, in the light of what we know about developing technology, we can see clearly at what kinds of jobs these people will be working, and from this deduce the new kinds of needs, both industrial and personal, which can arise. Looking at both occupation and recent trends, we can get insight into the

[2] Peter F. Drucker, *Managing for Results* (New York, Harper & Row, Publishers, 1964), page 135.

kinds of places and the regions where they will be living and from this learn of other needs that must be satisfied both directly and through governmental action. Looking at such occupational trends and recent trends in the demand for education, we can learn of probable new tastes as well as new institutional markets in which there will be developing room for many new kinds of volume production.

Likewise, the *new knowledge* that will be part of new saleable products ten and twenty years from now has already been born and is waiting only for perceptive enterprise to turn it into valuable market innovations. The growth firms of any period are those with the imagination to see the potential inherent in existing new knowledge already out of the laboratory and in published works of behavioral sciences and to translate these existent discoveries into saleable consumer benefits. One of the major international success stories of recent years has been the Japanese firm of Sony, which started with assets of only $530 in 1945 and built up to sales in 1963 of $77 million mostly by insight into the market possibilities opened up by the American development of the transistor. Yet when Masura Ibuka saw the personal pocket-size radio inherent in the transistor, it was a full six years after Bell Laboratories and Western Electric had released their research results to the world, and any number of American electronics producers could easily have beat him to the market had they possessed his insight into consumer needs. It took the imagination of a Chicago advertising executive to see the real potential in farm feed sales in the newer knowledge of antibiotic and vitamin additives in livestock feeds if made directly available to the farmer. The water-dispersible products business he developed was later purchased back by the drug industry itself for several million dollars.

Changes in industry and market structure have often proved the opportunity for the new business to by-pass the lead of established competitors. None of the early supermarkets were built by the major food chains of the early 1930's. They overlooked the changes wrought in the distribution of food by Detroit's major product and by the mechanical refrigerator. The unknown outsiders have come to dominate many of the regional markets of the country.

The ability of the supermarket to buy directly from large producers has, in turn, created opportunities for foresighted large farmers and progressive farm marketing groups to build premium markets for tailored farm produce developed around the need of large individual buyers. One eastern farm the author knew as a general operation much like its neighbors a generation ago today depends for a large share of a really large income on the production of a specific variety of the potato, planted, cared for, and stored at a temperature specifically designed to fit it for a single use: potato chips. This farm businessman's neighbors still run operations of a size similar to those of a generation ago, and for general markets, as they did. Their incomes are only a minor fraction of his.

Sometimes the useful product idea is not new to the world but only to the particular market, and the competitor who gets ahead is the one who sees *the applicability of the experience of older markets to the new one.* A British sales manager for a floor covering maker once told the author that his product planning procedure was quite simple—just look at the trend six months to a year earlier in the United States. Most lags are greater than this, of course. The electric refrigerators being sold in Europe when they began to sell in volume—in the late 1950's—had about the same storage capacity as those sold thirty years earlier in the United States, when the ice refrigerator was beginning to give real ground to the mechanical cooler and the supermarket was not quite a gleam in anyone's eye. In the reverse direction, there could be some cause for speculation as to whether Detroit could not learn something from the European automobile industry about the potentialities of the end of the automobile market that is highly individual in tastes and needs.

Looking at Product Weaknesses for Market-Winning Advantages. Management too often takes a fatalistic attitude toward the weaknesses that every product package contains and does nothing about them. If they view them as challenges rather than as inevitable weaknesses, they can frequently go beyond defending them from the competition to which they are vulnerable and open up market segments not previously in reach. Such service defects are usually of at least one of the following four types:

1. heavy initial investment cost
2. high use cost in monetary terms, or in effort or convenience of use
3. highly fluctuating quality, price, or both (usually true of natural raw materials).
4. esthetic defects such as appearance or odor.

High initial investment often frightens off prospects for product packages of admittedly high value for the total cost required. Even those who do buy continually look for acceptable substitutes with lower investment requirements. Industrial platinum is a good example. In its use as a catalyst for refining petroleum, as an acid-proof spinneret for rayon filament, and as a high-melting spinneret for glass fiber, no substitute material has proved as good, or as cheap. Moreover, the principal investment is a one-time thing. Worn spinnerets and catalysts can be reprocessed for a relatively small cost. But that investment is high, close to five million dollars for one spinneret user, for example. Consequently, every user is on a keen lookout for some cheaper substitute.

One successful avoidance of this initial investment barrier, for high-ticket consumer items such as houses and autos, has been the time payment plan.[3] Most habitual time payment buyers think only in terms of the size of the periodic payment. Industrial buyers sometimes find leasing less onerous. If the equipment itself is basically a promotional item to gain a market for supplies (as Gillette promotes razors to sell blades), the lease cost can even be kept attractively low relative to its investment value.

High use costs are usually shrugged off or ignored by sellers of items whose unit cost is low. Steel's cost per pound has always given it such a market advantage that the possible competition of

---

[3] Curiously enough, the sellers of a really large big-ticket consumer item of growing importance—a college education—still insist on pay-as-you-go for most buyers. They prefer to keep the price below the market value, making up deficit costs by going begging, and penalizing the employees, and probably product quality as a result, rather than ease the investment problem by making an adequate credit supply freely available and relatively painless, as the auto and appliance industries have. Meanwhile, the higher educational industry continues to wonder why so many of the "best" potential prospects do not buy.

lighter weight products was always considered a pipe dream by the industry—until container users started shifting to aluminum and even paper-and-foil combinations to save shipping cost. Then the steel industry suddenly discovered it could make a satisfactory lighter weight tin plate.

The promoters of bus-travel commuting have long held onto a belief, in the face of contrary evidence, that the commuter should appreciate the lower per-trip cost of the bus, compared with the personal automobile. But the commuter continues to abandon the busses the worse the traffic jam grows, because he saves precious time. Meanwhile mass-transit travelling on a privileged right-of-way has proved able to hold its own, and even gain, wherever the subways and commuter trains gave acceptable service otherwise, indicating that time cost is the important element.

Inconvenient shape for mechanical handling, and highly variable quality and size are typical weaknesses of natural raw materials, rendering their processing costly both in effort and money. Grading can help alleviate the quality problem at times, but more attention needs to be given to putting the materials into a form adaptable to automatic processing. One of the obvious attractions of Dupont's synthetic for shoe uppers, Corfam, is the fact that it can be bought in flawless rolls of uniform thickness and width, making automatic machine cutting and fabrication available to the shoe industry. Even at this late date, it would be well for the hide industry to develop some preprocessing of natural leather to give it these desired characteristics.

Esthetic weaknesses always present a major opportunity to capture virgin market segments and move out ahead of the industry, showing it the way to new markets. More usually, the whole industry tends to take them for granted as inherent, doing nothing until hit by strong outside competition by near-substitutes, as happened in the case of cotton.

The belief that "cotton is king" led the Southern Confederacy into a false belief that European customer countries would spring to its aid when it seceded from the Union. While the conclusion proved wrong, cotton was the mainstay of the world's textile industry with no visible competition of consequence until a decade after World War I. But if king it was, it had many unpopular

characteristics. It shrunk. When dyed, it had a dull look and the dyes ran. The result was a faded dress or shirt, maybe good enough to do hard labor in, or scrub floors, but not for dressing up.

Then out of nowhere came a laboratory fiber that had been around since 1894, but under the name of "artificial silk" had not gone anywhere. Rechristened "rayon," it began to get engineering support and, by the end of the '30's, had captured the dress market from silk, then began invading traditional cotton uses, at a price competitive with the latter, and with processing characteristics that were more uniform, backed up by technical assistance from the producers.

Fortunately for the industry, cotton producers and processors got together in the Cotton Council, discovered that many of the traditional weaknesses were not necessary, and developed, then promoted for high fashion use, cotton fabrics with little shrinkage, which dyed well and held their dyes. By the beginning of the 1950's, it had won a foothold in fashion garments it never had before, and was competing on equal terms with rayon in women's clothes. By dint of continuing innovation, the threat from newer synthetic fibers was met by new fabric finishes that reduced the need to iron garments, and also by development of cotton blends with synthetics which made use of the desirable feel of cotton while capturing the easy-care characteristics of the synthetics.

Some weaknesses really cannot be overcome, of course. High-tensile-strength rayon had such a clear superiority over cotton for tire cord that nothing could be done to save this market for cotton.

Waiting until others capture market segments before attacking product weaknesses reverses the natural advantage of the established seller. While he remains the source of supply for a segment, the consumption systems of the customers in that segment are built around the established seller's product. It takes a major benefit to win the customer to the point of paying the actual or emotional changeover cost. Once changed, however, the new product has the advantage, which must be overcome with a vastly greater value difference than would have been needed to hold the business in the first place.

Product Ideas Directly from the Customer. The customer would seem to be an obvious source of ideas which would give a firm preferred entree to his purse. For product modifications, he can be, with careful analytical research. But he is unlikely to be a fruitful source of ideas of dramatic revolutionary import because his consumption systems are guided by comfortable habit, and he tends to think in terms of something fitting these existing systems, and even existing design formats.

Because of customer conservatism, *direct questioning* concerning likes and dislikes in terms of total design configuration can never be trusted far. Interrogation must be in terms of the simplest components of designs, and analysis must be focussed on trends in attitudes. Just such a trend analysis of customer attitudes toward hair styles enabled a seller of home permanents to foresee a major change in the market demand pattern before it showed up in sales and to shift the brunt of a decline to competing producers.

What any such research seeks is a measure of the willingness to pay a price differential. The research should attempt a direct measure of this willingness, preferably by means of some form of *simulated purchase situation,* some research design that forces the respondent to make a choice in terms approaching a real purchase decision, such as lottery simulation. He may get a chance, for example, to win, in substantial quantity, the choice he names in a drawing.

With skilled analysis, *product-in-use* studies can reveal ways of adding a differential value to well-established product types by outlining in detail the consumption system used and permitting examination of the customer problems involved in that use. Such studies can also reveal how costs can be cut without cutting perceived customer benefits by indicating service elements in the product package not desired by the customer. Many products are overengineered in terms of what the consumer can discriminate or desires. The expert can usually appreciate values of no consequence to the user.

However the new product idea is developed, or how potentially valuable to the customer, it should not be offered until the firm determines whether it is one this particular firm has the skills and resources to exploit profitably. The firm should then confine production efforts to those parts of the package in the production of which it can excel competition.

Is This Product for Us?

Product differentiation is as much due to the differences in skills and resources of the sellers as to the different tastes and needs of major market segments. The limits on both the skills and resources of the firm limit the kind of product packages it can promote and the market segments it can serve better than others. Any successful firm carries out some services better than any close competitor, and the latter will excel in some other direction.

In the general mail-order industry, for example, Sears is acknowledged to excel in rational economic planning and in personnel handling (helping it achieve lower personnel costs). Ward's is given credit for such a superior job of merchandising that it upgraded the level of the whole industry, but its economic planning and personnel management were long the scandal of the industry. Alden's is credited with better and more efficiently streamlined physical operations than any of the other three. Spiegel's has long had the reputation of doing a more imaginative and profitable job of promoting the sale of credit and is said to have invented the *add-on* credit system, now generally known under the name of the revolving charge account. But the taste for the spectacular which helped it do this has interfered with its economic planning, and its lack of ability to develop autonomous local managers combined to make an entry into retail store operation less than profitable.

DO WE EXCEL IN THE PRODUCTION OF THE TOTAL SERVICE PACKAGE?

Every proposed innovation requires a close look at the match between those skills at which the firm excels and the service elements it needs to produce to build up the desired consumer values. While most firms think of their skills largely in terms of physical product types, or sometimes types of distribution channels, their real skills usually prove to cut across physical product lines and channels of distribution.

A very successful toiletries firm (shampoos, hair and skin lotions, etc.) decided it could profitably expand into the seemingly closely related cosmetics field with lines sold through the same sorts of outlets, seemingly appealing to the same kinds of customer desires (personal appearance). Only after an initial entry into lipsticks failed to get off the ground did the firm discover that the promotional elements of the cosmetics products packages depended much less on the advertising pull at which it excelled and much more on the personal sales push of manufacturer-trained sales clerks, an area in which it had no experience or particular skill.

By contrast, when an attempt to follow the aircraft industry into rocket part production failed for a metal-working firm that had been a dominant supplier of precision parts, it found a market in a quite different direction—in a contract for a volume run of firearms whose precision requirements were giving Army Ordnance a major production headache. Its skill, the executives discovered, lay in their knowledge of metallurgy and in translation of this knowledge into low-cost production of long runs of precision metal parts. Rocket parts production did not fit; the production runs were too short.

Sometimes, of course, the firm can take on only that part of the package production at which it excels and must farm out the parts others can do better. Nearly the whole of industry does this with its advertising, for example. Polaroid essentially produces only the design and sales promotion elements of its unique cameras. Both the instrument and film are made by others.

DO WE HAVE THE REQUIRED RESOURCES?

Any innovational package must not only match the skills of the firm, but must require no more of the financial sinews and the resources of executive time and energy than are available. Some of the need for both can be decreased by getting others to take on part of the production, physical or otherwise, but others are unlikely to take on the costly and high-risk portions of the package, particularly those most demanding of top executive attention over prolonged periods. The depth of resources needed and the period of their need will depend on the degree of psychological innovation being attempted. This psychological scale is best described in terms of its two extremes:

1. evolutionary modifications of existing service systems, fitting perfectly those aspects of present consumption systems that are not inherently annoying to the customer
2. revolutionary service packages, requiring a complete reorganization of customer consumption systems, changes in his viewpoint and understanding, or both.

Only modest resources are needed to develop the potential of *evolutionary innovations* that add materially to perceived value without disturbing the market segment's consumption systems, no matter how radically different the physical product is technologically. The chemistry of synthetic detergents differed materially from that of the laundry soaps they displaced, but the housewife only needed to know they could be substituted in her washing machine for a better result without change of procedure. She welcomed the first ones with such open arms as to change the producers' conception that they had a product simply for hard water areas. Similarly, black-and-white television was a major engineering break-through, but to the consumer simply a more convenient form of the familiar movies, i.e., movies in the parlor; it never had to be sold—it was bought on sight. The locational element that was new had a high added value for families with children.

Educating the customer to appreciate the need and the values for him in the changes in his habitual consumption systems required by the *revolutionary innovation* inevitably calls for prolonged investment of time and energy and strong financial resources. Initially, such systems have no perceived value for any sizeable market segment, or at least very little, and potential consumers must be taught to see the latent values. Color television has been just such a case. Few consumers saw any value in the color picture to justify the necessarily higher price of the receiver. RCA spent tens of millions of dollars and ten years of effort in a long educational and promotional campaign before the public began to buy in profitable volume.

Such a revolutionary innovation may seem like a minor one technologically. The public's acceptance of frozen soup concentrates was well established when Campbell introduced its frozen fruit soup. But fruit, in soup form, served cold, moreover, did not fit the American food consumption system, and fruit soup was still-born.

Product-Line Competition

Many firms start with a single physical product, but most sooner or later develop groups or lines of products for various reasons, and their real product becomes the line itself. Product management then becomes the management of the interrelationships of a changing complex which has its own rationale separate from that of the individual elements, and the whole needs continuous review as to its composition and the allocation of executive attention and resources to achieve the greatest competitive efficiency.

PRODUCT LINE STRUCTURE DECISIONS

Product lines may initially develop for financial, production, or market reasons, or for a combination of these.

1. Financial reasons. Production and/or sale of a diverse line may permit the sharing and thus the reduction of the burden of fixed costs of administration, production, and sales.
2. Production reasons. Products with complementary seasonal or cyclical sales patterns can stabilize earnings and operations.
3. Market reasons.
   a. Market needs are too diverse and the pattern perhaps too shifting to be met with a single model or very limited number of models.
   b. The customer needs an assortment of related items and prefers the economy of a limited number of sources.

Lines put together solely for financial or production reasons would result in lower costs and thus some competitive advantage in themselves, but nearly every line has market reasons behind its structure also. In fact, where the savings of joint cost are in selling, the line must be a market reason line also—the constituent items must all meet the assortment needs of a segment or closely related group of market segments, and be sold in the same way.

Lines of varying models of the same general class of physical product are common in both the industrial and the consumer fields. The obvious consumer case is that of the automobile industry. In the early days when a large segment of the market wanted mainly basic transportation, the elder Henry Ford could get by with a single model of his trailbreaking T, in black. His grandson, to get the trade of a large enough group of related segments, has to offer such a diversity of body types, chassis, color choices, and accessory combinations that he might conceivably operate one of his smaller assembly plants for a year without repeating. The market today has a highly segmented demand which can shift radically in pattern from one year to the next. One year, the heavy demand may be for deluxe models for V-8 engines. The 6-cylinder models with modest decoration may dominate purchases the next year. Such a diverse line and the goodwill backlog built up also ease the problem of introducing new product variants appealing to new market segments. To a considerable degree, the line name becomes an important element of consumer value among diverse groups, separate from the goodwill attached to a particular group of models. This implies, of course, that the firm must stick to introduction of new elements that fit the image the other elements in the line have constructed, in other words, fit the values of the market segments attracted by previous products.

For many sellers, both of consumer and industrial goods, the assortment itself is the only basis of differentiation and the only method of meeting the needs of a particular segment or closely related groups of segments. Individual items would be available from a number of other sellers, but not in the same kind of assortment, and the customer prefers to keep his sources limited. Both U. S. Steel and Crucible are steel makers, but their assortments and customers are quite different. The assortment offered gains preference by meeting the needs of a very specific segment of potential customers whose desired goods and services are heavily overlapping and who normally buy in the same way. In such a line, those product elements should be included which:

1. are sold to the same market segments, the same buying level, as the other items in the line, supplementing the desired assortments of the same customers
2. meet the special needs of a closely related group of segments better than the assortment of any other seller
3. are sold by the same means, through the same channels.

ALLOCATING RESOURCES TO THOSE ELEMENTS GIVING THE GREATEST DIFFERENTIATION

The aim of product line management is to devote the greatest amount of executive attention and promotional resources to those elements that give the market segment the greatest differenial value, and thus return the greatest incremental profit for each unit of time and money spent. Inevitably, these items will change in identity constantly, and they will always be the up-and-coming items in the line. For, as emphasized throughout, products have their greatest differentiation early in their life cycle, before competition duplicates and improves upon them. Any review of the items in a line would do well to try fitting all into one of the classifications Peter Drucker has proposed.[4]   His main classification consists of eleven categories, of which the first five are simple of diagnosis and easy to decide how to treat, the other six, problem children:

1. *today's breadwinners*—accounting for today's market advantage as shown by the profit in their sale, but soon to be matched or improved upon by competitors' offerings, and thus losing their differential advantage
2. *tomorrow's breadwinners*—already adding to the firm's competitive advantage, as shown by their wide acceptance in large and profitable volume, but with the main growth foreseeably ahead, and the chance to become a market leader with proper attention
3. *productive specialties*—serving a limited but distinct market seg-

[4] Peter F. Drucker, *Managing for Results* (New York, Harper & Row, Publishers, 1964), p. 51-67.

ment which values them highly; net revenue contribution proportionately higher than their volume, employing limited resources, and contributing a disproportionately low share of cost burden

4. *development products*—not really products yet, but with prospects of serving the special desires of a well-defined market segment substantially better than anything available

5. *obvious failures*

6. *yesterday's breadwinners*—sales still large, but no longer offering any differential value to customers as evidenced by the price cuts and excessive sales expense needed to maintain sales, at the expense of profit contribution

7. *repair job*—suffering from one and only one defect in the satisfaction package; already has substantial preference with an important market segment, promising growth potential, a significant leadership position, and a high probability of success if the defect is corrected

8. *unnecessary specialties*—existence of a number of special products where one main product could meet those needs the market segment values

9. *unjustified specialties*—a differentiation in which the customer sees no proportionate value, and will not pay

10. *investments in managerial ego*—the product that management is sure deserves success, but has found no extensive market segment which accords it a preferential value; does serve a limited market segment, so that failure is not blatantly obvious, but great enough to drain profits and resources

11. *cinderellas or sleepers*—products capable of better serving the desires of a substantial market segment than anything available, but whose potential is overlooked because it competes with today's breadwinner, or whose total profit is overlooked because unit percentage is low, the sales organization not fitted to promote it, or other reasons without economic validity.

To this classification needs to be added a twelfth implicit in his discussion:

12. *the product that is not really a product at all, but a form of sales promotion for some other product.* The obvious recognized case is the Gillette razor, which is really a promotional device to sell Gillette blades—the profit product. There are many others, not all of them recognized as such. Their distinguishing mark is that the

more they sell, the more profit the firm makes on the sale of some related item. Their own cost and profit is thus irrelevant to price, or to any decision to promote or drop.

The strongest market position will be attained by the firm that milks yesterday's breadwinners of whatever profit they have, then drops them; puts just enough effort behind today's breadwinners to maintain momentum; and devotes its best talent and resources to tomorrow's breadwinners, the cinderellas, and to a lesser extent (until proved) the day-after-tomorrow's breadwinners, the development product. Productive specialties would get adequate but limited support to retain the preference of the limited market segment served. Repair jobs would be given one good chance to prove that all they need in order to get the preference of the target segment is to correct the single defect in physical characteristics, in channel of sale, or whatever it is conceived to be.

By thus concentrating its energies and resources in those areas in which it can create real added value for substantial market segments, the firm can get an incremental profit out of each dollar and executive hour spent.

Summary

1. The market definition of product as every element of value for which the customer will pay has to be understood if competitive strategy is to yield the optimum profit. Variation in product characteristics is the principal weapon of strategy. Distinction must be made between the market product and the physical product. The latter is only an element of the total, and may be included in more than one market product, depending on the service elements in the product package valued by different market segments.

2. Competition is multidimensional, containing some aspects of monopoly, some of competition. For a core segment of the market which values highly all of the important differentiating elements in the total product package offered, the seller has a monopoly. But for those segments who value only the elements in common between his product and those of close competitors, he is in open competition with these sellers of close substitutes, at a

price level comparable to the customer's perception of the value of these common elements. The differential value of the unique elements in the different packages offered may well be quite different in customer value, with some so great as to make concentration on the core market advisable. Each product will share different package components with different kinds of products, so that close competitors in one direction may not be in competition at all with other close competitors in another direction. The ultimate measure of competition is substitutibility at a given price, for a given market segment.

3. This consumer-oriented model of competition puts the emphasis on constant innovation, rather than on price as the key to competitive success as does traditional physical-product-oriented static economic analysis. It requires understanding of the customer's perception of the product for correct planning, and recognizes that such perceptions of value change over time, that all innovation grants only temporary advantage because what one firm can do, another can copy and improve upon. It also recognizes that innovation is broader than mere physical invention, that the valuable differentiating elements may well lie entirely outside the physical product, in accompanying technical advice, or in better-designed promotion.

4. The most profitable new products are to be sought in providing missing elements that make available whole new technologies. It is also fruitful to analyze that part of the future whose seeds are visible in the present: population trends that will grow out of today's population structure, new knowledge developments not yet translated into marketable products, changes in market and industry structure that make inevitable new product needs, and the experience in other markets which may foreshadow changes in your own. Other product ideas can be found by analyzing weaknesses in your own current product offering. Finally, imaginative probing of the customer can lead to profitable new product ideas.

5. Every new product must be assessed for its suitability for the firm in the light of the firm's special knowledge and for the kinds of resources needed to develop its market potential. Special attention must be directed to the extent to which this development

requires the customer to adopt new consumption systems, in which case the firm will have to look forward to heavy investment in financial and executive resources.

6. In the end, most product decisions must be decisions on the proper management of a product line and the proper allocation of resources to those elements in the line which will generate increasing business in the future.

5

Price: The Tactical Weapon
of Competition

FOR THE SELLER, price is the basic tool of day-to-day competitive tactics. Of all the tools in the marketing arsenal, only price can be put into effect on a moment's notice to achieve surprise.

Price is also the one economic concept most of us understand, even when we are unclear as to what we are paying it for. It is a simple sum of money given as a consideration for some product or service. The pricing decision itself, however, is far from simple. The *latitude for price decision* open to a firm is limited by industry patterns, customs, and buyer attitudes. However much it may seem on the surface to be administered, price is really the buyer's tool. His willingness to pay it is a powerful incentive to induce sellers to bring forth the service packages he desires. Even though the response of supply to the buyer's willingness to pay is not as prompt as the response of competitors to price cuts, in the end, it is usually as certain.

Pricing decisions are really of three types:

1. the basic price level decision
2. price structure decisions (This involves decisions as to the relationship between prices in a product line, and decisions as to the structure of the discounts used in the distribution chain. The latter are essentially prices paid for selling services, and the decision is basically a buying decision.)
3. decisions on temporary price competitive tactics.

Distinction must be made between the static aspects of price and the dynamic aspects of the price decision. Static price theory can be a poor guide for pricing decisions in a dynamic business situation. Recognition must also be given to the existence of moralistic concepts of pricing: concepts centering around the general idea of *fair price*.

The Latitude for Price Decision and Its Method of Expression

Those outside of management tend toward easy overestimation of the amount of discretion executives can exercise in setting a price. Even among many of the economically sophisticated, the expression *setting a price* and its technical synonym, *administered pricing*, conjure up a vision of arbitrary action which ignores the readily observable facts of everyday shopping.

To a very considerable extent, it is the buyer rather than the seller who sets the price and determines its mode of expression. Price is the crowbar the buyer uses to pry out of some seller the product package he wants, or perhaps, more accurately, the carrot he dangles in front of business to get some hungry competitor to go his way with product characteristics.

It is probable, of course, that many a harried price manager doing his best to respond to competitive pressures somewhat overstates the rigidities of the limitation upon his price discretion. These limitations are very real, however, and their character depends upon the industry and the particular product package the manager is trying to peddle. Any industry and product situation fits into one of several distinct classes:

1. uniform price situations of one of two types: (a) traditional price levels, or (b) uniform competitive prices
2. price line situations
3. target pricing situations aimed at: (a) percentage profit margin on sales, (b) percentage return on investment, or (c) break-even-plus pricing
4. bid price situations
5. truly differentiated price situations.

These situation types are not mutually exclusive. The uniform price situation consisting of a traditional price class may really be one of several price line classes and conceal a true form of differentiated price or differential product.

UNIFORM INDUSTRY PRICING: TRADITIONAL PRICES

A pack of chewing gum was five cents in 1905 and still is in 1965. Except under recognized discount operations, and then usually only in terms of multi-unit purchases, regular brands of candy bars must be priced at either a nickel or a dime. This was true in 1925 and remained true in 1965. It would be folly to try to offer a candy bar at 7 cents.

However, this price stability is somewhat illusory, particularly in the case of the candy bar, although not the chewing gum. The price *per package* may remain stable, or may have to jump from 5 cents to 10 cents, but the amount of *product sold per cent* can and does vary. Bar sizes are changed, and sometimes also the quantity of the more expensive ingredients. Nevertheless, the consumer, even before the widespread use of the vending machine, seems to insist that the price of the bar be at one of these fixed points, regardless of the quantity of candy therein. At any one time, moreover, management has relatively little discretion about the weight of the candy in the bar. Regardless of the wide differentiation in types of bars, customers seem to expect a relatively similar size. In a very real sense, this is really a customer-dictated price-line situation even when there is only a single price line, as in stick chewing gum.

UNIFORM INDUSTRY PRICING: COMPETITIVE PRICES

A much more widespread form of uniform industry pricing typifies industries with relatively undifferentiated products. If the seller hopes to make any sales, he cannot hope to get a higher price than his competitors in the same outlet. There is no added consumer value. Thus, all detergents of the same class in the supermarket normally carry the same price tag (except possibly the private brand of the store). It makes little difference to the clerk at the check-out whether you picked up Tide or Surf or Fab or Ajax; she rings up the same price on the register. The products need not be identical physically. It must only be that consumer loyalty is low enough so that a slight difference in price can cause a substantial shift to another brand. The most successful product gets its reward in terms of the patronage of a larger market segment.

Similarly, if you buy steel for your factory, you will pay the same price for your raw materials whether you buy from United States Steel, Bethlehem, or Jones and Laughlin. This is in no sense evidence that these three steelmakers (and the others) are conspiring against you. They simply are aware that they cannot retain the loyalty of a given customer if they attempt to charge him a higher price than does some competitor. Nor is it a sign that they are selling completely undifferentiated products. In physical specifications, there will be no difference in the steel. But in terms of customer service, there probably will be some. You may have chosen the supplier you use because of the especially good service his salesman renders. You will not, however, stand for paying a higher price for his product than for somebody else's. Again, differentiation's reward is a preferred position with a larger segment of the market, rather than premium price.

Indeed, in all uniform industry situations, profit must come from lower cost in delivering the total product to the customer. As J. M. Clark would put it, cost becomes the major variable of competition in such a case.

ENGINEERING A PRODUCT TO A PRICE LINE

If you go shopping with your wife along the main stem of your shopping district and make a frequency distribution of the prices of women's dresses, blouses, and skirts—or of the various men's garments, for that matter—you find all prices grouped at certain precise points, with no prices quoted in between. Dresses on any rack would be either $7.95, $8.95, $11.95 or the like, but none would be $7.69, $8.29, or any other intermediate price. This is the way the ready-made garment industry has operated for many decades, and both merchants and customers seem to prefer it this way. In such a situation, the only price decision the manufacturer can make is to determine at which price-line point he can do best. He must then *engineer the cost and construction* of his output to hew as closely as possible to the standards required of this line. Since every competitor selling at that particular level must do the same, this means a close shaving of costs indeed to meet the critical eye of the merchandise buyer. If he cannot meet the quality standards at that price, the seller must engineer his product for a price-line whose requirements he can meet. His choice is a product choice, not a price choice.

The case of gasoline is similar. You will either buy a major brand at one given price, standard for every station in your area, or you will buy a cut-rate brand at a lower level (most likely, 2 cents per gallon less). The gasoline itself may be physically identical in both cases, but the service of the cut-rate supplier will be tailored to keep costs down to the lower level. For example, he will choose high-traffic locations only and put major emphasis on fuel sales rather than on added forms of service such as lubrication.

Whatever the form of uniform industry pricing, the seller in such a situation can use price solely as a very temporary tactical maneuver such as the "eight cents off" package of detergents when a competitor's minor differentiation requires some temporary defense; the "two for little more than the price of one" used to get introductory sampling, or some other form of "deal"; or a Trip-to-Europe contest for those sending in the bottle caps, or baseball cards in the bubblegum package. Care has to be exercised to see that such temporary devices do not become incorporated into the product as a permanently expected feature and an additional item of cost which must be sustained to keep the customer purchasing at the same price others can get without this new product element (as has happened with coupons on cigarette packages, special offers on cereal boxes, etc.).

The only escape from such uniform industry-wide prices to higher levels when needed is to find a distribution channel reaching an isolated market segment with a service element, e.g., in-home selling, not offered by others. A maker of American bone china who ran into difficulty competing with less expensive imports in ordinary retail outlets raised both prices and total sales by developing a house-to-house sales operation dealing with the very special market segment that responds well to this sales technique.

TARGET PRICING

Uniform prices occur because the value of possible substitutes is so close to that of the firm's product that buyers will not willingly pay more for it. At the other extreme stand products which differ so much from possible competing substitutes that management not only is relatively free to quote a price, but has no market price to guide it in making a quotation. Such, for example, would be the case of revolutionary new products whose total service package is radically different from any now available to buyers, e.g., nylon filament when first introduced, a new drug with therapeutic properties in advance of anything available for a disease entity hitherto difficult to treat, a new piece of literature, or a textbook with a really different treatment of a subject (which all claim to have). How price such items? The answer that is almost universally used in industry is some form of target pricing.

There are really three kinds of targets used in this approach: (1) cost plus a predetermined margin, (2) return on investment, and (3) break-even-plus.

Whenever the fixed investment required is not additional and specific to the particular product, the tendency, apparently, is to price on a *cost-plus-a target profit* basis, and the target profit is very frequently 10 percent. Such may also be the procedure where substantial and specific fixed investment is involved, but the costing in that case really implies a great deal of faith in some aspect of the estimation of market potential. This is also the method of making the initial price estimate on custom production, with some standard allowance for overhead and administration, as in job shop operations. Such price estimates, however, are subject to adjustment on the basis of the market situation for the custom manufacture services involved. In essence, the profit margin quoted in such cases is really a uniform industry price for custom production service. An interesting question arises as to why 10 percent target profit. The answer seems to be that this is a level acceptable to both sellers and buyers, that is, a "fair price" psychologically from the buyer's standpoint (*see* discussion of fair price attitudes on the buyer's part, below).

Return-on-investment pricing on revolutionary new products is basically a form of investment decision rather than a pricing decision. To make the calculation, some estimate must be made as to the minimum market expected over the minimum life of the investment. Some estimate of the prices chargeable in view of the value package being offered to the most likely market segments must also be made. If the discounted cash flow estimated from this possible price and the estimated sales to be developed exceed the target selected after taxes, the tendency would be to approve the investment. If the price indicated by careful analysis seems well above the 10 percent-return level, based on only the most visible potential markets, the decision is easy; the price set at the 10 percent-return level can be expected to open less immediately apparent markets.

Return-on-investment pricing is also used for some kinds of established products, estimating the market at some standard volume. Such is the practice of the automobile industry. In any industry with a highly fluctuating demand from year-to-year, such standard-cost- and return-on-investment pricing seems to be the only rational rule yet devised, and has done much to help build General Motors into the profitable giant it is.

Use of such a return-on-investment price does mean foregoing a temporarily acceptable price in boom periods and undoubtedly leads to black market operations in severe booms such as the auto industry experienced after World War II. But it should be noted that it does help maintain the goodwill of a customer whose regular return is essential to the firm's health. In the case of the auto industry, for example, the ultimate retail price is a complex negotiated barter; GM's quotation to the dealer is the only price it really sets.

Unless something like an estimate of the market is available, or no substantial costs are fixed, neither of the above methods are possible bases for price decision. For instance in book publishing, a very substantial investment must be made before a single copy is sold, in editorial labor, typesetting, and distribution of free review copies—large numbers of them in the case of a textbook. Furthermore, a considerable overhead must be maintained in the constant search for authors and potential authors. This is as much a part of the job of the salesforces as the pushing of books already issued. The estimate of the potential acceptance of any given manuscript is highly conjectural. At best, an editor can make some minimum estimate, but none could honestly foresee that a particular work in government used at the freshman level would dominate the market, in various editions, from 1922 until 1965 (as one has proved). While the adoption of a text may be influenced somewhat by price because professors (even of economics) tend toward a "right price" concept much like ordinary humans, the choice of a text is based primarily on product characteristics, not on the price of dissimilar books covering the same subject.

The *break-even target* is the publisher's answer, and it is the only one that makes sense for anyone faced with such conjectural estimates of probable market size. The responsible editor makes the best possible estimate of the minimum number he can hope to sell in the very short run and prices to break even on all start-up and production costs for this minimum quantity. If his judgment of manuscripts and markets is good, he will make a very small profit on most manuscripts, lose on very few or none, and, with luck, pick a few classics which turn in increasing profits as the years go by.

Target return methods have inherent dangers which must be watched, especially when used in connection with pricing of established products. It is easy to forget about latent potential competition and set prices so high as to bring this competition into actuality. It is easy to lose sight of the necessity for a constant vigil concerning costs, especially capital cost. Thus the tendency of the steel industry in the post World War II era to use target-return pricing caused it to overlook the possibility of increasing potential competition from other materials and the consequent need to find ways of reducing the heavy investment needed per ton of production. Prices were steadily boosted until 1957 to cover costs of the new old-style high cost capacity until sudden inroads of aluminum, prestressed concrete, and plastics aroused the industry to its dangers and forced it to perfect and put into operation much less costly oxygen reduction processes, the possibility of which had been there all along.

TRULY DIFFERENTIATED PRICING: COMPLEX STANDARD PRODUCTS

When differentiation tends to be viewed by the buyer as a matter of single-dimensional quality differences, price line differentiation tends to be the pattern. But differentiation in physically complex products usually is multidirectional, so no clear quality statements are possible. (What is the relative quality grade of the Buick and Chrysler automobiles, for example?) Each seller of such a product is producing for his own special core market segment, with some overlapping of fringe segments between sellers. Quite usually in such cases, the customer has considerable option as to the exact mixture of physical characteristics in the package bought from a given manufacturer, especially in capital equipment and in consumer durables such as automobiles and refrigerators. Typically, the list price quoted by the seller includes physical options most buyers want, but the accessories that are considered part of the standard package by one manufacturer will differ from those included in a competing seller's standard package, with prices of optional accessories differing from seller to seller partly by reason of actual design and cost differences in the optional equipment.

Buyers, particularly in the in-between fringe segments from which added sales are to be won, do make some kind of price comparisons, and the problem is to determine on what basis these comparisons are made. In some cases, it is on the basis of some central component of the physical product package being sold, very seldom on the basis of the total cost of the complete package. The automobile dealer, for example, advertises the suggested factory price of his "stripped model"—a Chevrolet, for example—for $1945. He expects to get very few customers who really want this particular package, but hopes (usually correctly) that the customer will not compare the total cost of the kind of package he has in mind (perhaps $3002) with similar competing packages, not identical in any case. Similarly, a farmer buying a tractor may compare only the base price of the tractor itself, without the power steering, plows, and other attachments he will purchase with it. He will then judge the cost of these other components on what he thinks to be a fair price for the particular accessory, *as designed for this particular tractor.*

On the other hand, the price comparison may ignore the cost of the original physical package and be concerned with cost of the maintenance service components after purchase. A secretarial teacher commented that she was not interested in the price quotation on a certain piece of office equipment because, with her operation, she had many service calls, and the make she had been using was quite good about sending out service men without cost to her, whereas other companies billed her a substantial minimum fee for each call.

If the price comparison is on the basis of some central component, the seller needs first to determine what part of the package forms the basis of comparison and how it is compared. For accessories and attachments, he then should know what price looks fair from the buyer's point of view. At a time when the power steering extra on most tractors was selling for around $150 to $200, one of the makers brought out a very simplified design that worked very well, on his particular tractor. But he decided the customer would not, in view of its obvious simplicity, pay more than $20 or $25 extra for his edition, and so he incorporated it directly into the basic package.

Sometimes the package component that forms the basis of price comparison may be a relatively small fraction of the value of the normal package sold. Whether or not the accounting indicates a "satisfactory" profit margin on this one component is immaterial; the only relevant costing is the profit on the entire package. When Gillette first introduced the adjustable razor, the research department is said to have submitted two alternatives for price decision, one optimizing profit on the razor, the other optimizing total sales. Management chose the latter on the basis that its main interest was in the sale of blades and that the holder was, in effect, part of the sales promotion for blades.

TRULY DIFFERENTIATED PRICING: BID PRICES

The pricing situations so far discussed imply that the seller determines product specifications, whether they are physical specifications or psychological performance. But a very considerable fraction of the economic activity centers around markets in which the buyer sets the specifications and invites the seller to name a price, e.g., nearly all construction; most major special items procured by governments (such as defense material); and large volume purchases by manufacturers, institutions, and governmental bodies.

In developing his bid, the seller must make three basic decisions, usually in the following order of importance:

1. What is the relative importance of profit and certainty in getting the business?
2. What is the estimated probability of each possible bid, for each competitor?
3. What special advantages do any of the bidders, including himself, have in securing this contract?

The answer to the first of these points will usually be based on a balancing out of three factors:

1. Given his backlog and immediate prospects, how important is it to get in more work to hold his organization intact?
2. Is this particular job the kind at which his organization excels?
3. Will the winning of this bid lead to additional profitable business in the future?

The appetite of a firm for a given piece of business will obviously be determined by its present hunger for business to survive. Nearly every organization has certain kinds of jobs it prefers, and others it would rather let someone else do (unless, of course, it gets a greater than usual profit margin). If the organization is wise, its preferences stem from experiences that have taught the executives at which special tasks it excels.

The question as to whether the winning bid can be expected to serve as an entering wedge to additional profitable business later needs very careful investigation and analysis, particularly in the bidding of initial or prototype units for a projected long series of future units, e.g., the bidding on the prototype for a military cargo plane. Sometimes the winning bid is for a special design of the successful firm's own, thus putting unsuccessful bidders at a disadvantage in securing the following production runs. But if most firms in the industry are hungry enough, it need not follow that all such business in the future will be at a nice profit. Thus, when objectives are being decided upon, some probability estimate must be made as to later actions of others in bidding for the production runs.

Whatever estimate of the situation is made, the firm's bid will be in one of three directions:

1. a bid set to get the business at a loss—a substantial one if need be—to get a foot in the door on future runs
2. a bid on which the company can hope to break even, or close to it, either to keep the organization in being, or in hope of future business on other contracts
3. a bid expected to yield a profit.

In all cases, the expected profit or loss should be discounted by the degree of probability of landing the bid, based on the best information available on the likely action of competitors.

Estimating Probable Profit. Logical *competitive bidding strategy* requires estimation of the probable profit from a bid proposal by multiplying the actual estimate of profit by the probability of landing the job at that bid. The estimate of the probability of landing the job is partly subjective, partly an objective analysis of past experience with each of the competitors faced. The subjectivity enters in determining what past experience is applicable to the current situation.

EXHIBIT 5-1. A Hypothetical Example of a Competitive Bidding Situation

Problem: You have been invited to bid on the control instrumentation for the first 5 out of an eventual program for building 59 submarplanes of radical new design. Your engineering has estimated your cost for your planned installation at $104,900 per vehicle. You are bidding against 3 competitors against whom you have bid for various kinds of jobs in the past, winning sometimes, sometimes losing to one or the other of them. A study of these past bidding situations during periods when business in your industry was at about the same moderate level as now reveals the following experience concerning the relationship of these competitors' bids when they won, as compared to your cost estimates (C) on the same jobs:

EXHIBIT 5-1.   (Cont.)

Competing Firm	Number of known bids	Number of bids won at C plus								
		8%	10%	12%	14%	15%	16%	17%	18%	19%
Unique Mach. Wks.	10	1		1	3	3		1		1
Twin Engrg. Corp.	6			1		4			1	
Trey Designers	9		1		2	4	1		1	

CUMULATIVE FREQUENCY OF COMPETITORS

Per cent of bids at or less than

	7%*	8%	10%	12%	14%	15%	16%	17%	18%	19%*
Unique	1	10	10	20	50	80	80	90	90	99
Twin	1	1	1	17	17	67	67	67	99	99
Trey	1	1	11	11	33	78	89	89	99	99

* Although no past bids were as low as 7% nor as high as 19%, it is only realistic to assume there is a small nominal probability that bids such as this, close to the range of those experienced, will occur, say, 1 chance in 100 when past experience is as limited as shown here.

ESTIMATED ACTUAL AND EXPECTED PROFIT FROM POSSIBLE BIDS ON THE 5 SUBMARPLANES WITH COST (C) ESTIMATED AT $104,900

Note: Since the bidders are independent, the probability of winning with a particular bid is the cumulative probability of winning against each of the other bidders in turn, as indicated by the calculation.

Bid Price	Profit, if won $	%	Probability of Winning	Expected Value of Profit
$111,250	$7350	7	$.99 \times .99 \times .99 = .97$	$7140
113,300	8400	8	$.9 \ \times .99 \times .99 = .89$	7470
115,390	10,490	10	$.9 \ \times .99 \times .89 = .79$	8280
117,489	12,589	12	$.8 \ \times .83 \times .89 = .59$	7440
119,586	14,686	14	$.5 \ \times .83 \times .67 = .28$	4110
120,735	15,835	15	$.2 \ \times .33 \times .22 = .015$	238

Bids above this level will have a negligible chance of success and negligible expected profit.

EXHIBIT 5-1. (Cont.)

Conclusions: If the firm's objective is optimum expected profit, then we should bid $115,390 per vessel, even though in this particular instance there is about 1 chance in 5 that we will not land at this figure.

Note that a bid of $117,489 is about as profitable in terms of expected levels as one of $113,300, and if won would pay off much better in dollars of profit *now*. Furthermore, the chance of landing the contract at this figure is about 3 in 5.

Exhibit 5-1 is a simplified illustration of the competitive bidding strategy approach. The logic of this approach is as follows:

1. It is assumed that every firm making a bid first estimates its cost, then adds some target percentage for profit. Normally it will have a fixed target percentage in mind, but the amount actually quoted will vary according to the firm's felt need for new business.
2. Any one competitor's estimate procedures are unlikely to lead to the same precise figures as your own but, in general, the differences between any one competitor's estimates and your own will tend to be consistent. Thus, if you have your own estimate on the job, your competitor's bid can be expressed as your cost, C, plus some percentage, c.
3. At any given level of anxiety for a job, therefore, each competitor's bids will show a reasonably consistent relationship to your cost C, and his past bids will have a definite frequency distribution centering around $C + c$ and looking much like any other cumulative probability distribution.
4. If you know what each competitor has done in the past under similar levels of industry activity, you can thus make an estimate, for each one for whom you have past information, of the probability that he will make a bid of any given size. From this you can build a table like the last one in Exhibit 5-1 and thus get a statement of the probable *long-run* profit to be expected from any given bid.

Note that the figures in the last column represent the *long-run profit experience* that will result from a given bidding procedure, assuming that past information about each competitor is a reliable guide to his behavior. The actual profit, *if* you win, will be that in the second column, of course. But it is not certain that you will win.

Do you automatically bid the optimum profit figure—$115,390 in the illustration? Not if your objective is something else, e.g., maximum likelihood of landing the job, or a desire for a maximum profit if taken on regardless of the probability of winning. In the latter case, you might well bid $120,000 and might conceivably win, although the chance of doing so is very small on the basis of the best knowledge you have available.

Price Structure Decisions

The seller's pricing decision is concerned most commonly with a number of products in a product line and usually with prices at several levels between the maker and the final buyer, seldom with a single product or product package at a single point in distribution, except in auction or bid pricing. His interest is in the price mix yielding the greatest profit to the whole operation, not the profit from a single item. This profit is a product of the weighted average of the line and the volume of goods the later sellers move, partly in response to the margins his discount structure gives them.

PRODUCT LINE PRICE STRUCTURES

Product line is a term used to cover two different types of product mixes: (1) complementary and supplementary items which the seller groups into an assortment that his particular market segment desires, in essence, a single product, the assortment itself, and (2) a group of nearly-exclusive buyer choices to serve a group of closely related market segments. Thus a steel mill will produce a lot of different types and sizes of bars, angles, sheets, structurals, and so forth, of different alloys and different working characteristics, because any buyer of steel needs an assortment of types and shapes and wants them from a single source. Chevrolet, on the other hand, may offer you a choice between four different basic chassis designs, a number of body types in each, quite a few options in the amount of trim and upholstery, and quite a number of combinations and permutations of paint colors, well knowing you are unlikely to buy more than one, but also that no single combination of these attributes will satisfy a very large market segment.

In either case, the product mix will be managed, or merchandised, so that a considerable market segment will have available the particular assortments desired, and also so that there will be no items in the line in which this segment has little interest. In pricing the line, some target-weighted margin will be selected, but this will correspond to the actual margin on any one item only by coincidence. Some items will be priced at a very low profit margin to make the company look inexpensive, others at a very attractive margin because the buyers are quite willing to pay a very profitable price for the items with the particular attribute of those items.

In the case of the mutually exclusive type of line, the seller will probably so structure his prices that a low-cost "stripped" model, which is relatively unattractive to the market segment served, carries a price ticket that looks relatively attractive compared to the low price of competitors. Items thought to have the greatest volume potential will probably be priced close to his profit target; items above them in the line yield substantially fatter profit margins.

Management of a line that is a customer assortment is somewhat more complex. Consider, for example, the case of a hypothetical maker of fine chemicals, with several hundred items in his catalog, reviewing his assortment:

Some items which sell in considerable quantity are price footballs. They are also an element of considerable significance in the cost structure of the customer.

A large number of items are sold in small volume, and the customer buys only a few dollars worth per year—at most, several hundred dollars worth. They constitute no significant element in the cost structure of these customers.

Some items are commodities whose prices are closely watched as barometers of price movements and indicators of competitive price position in the trade.

Some items are being sold at a loss to customers who purchase sizeable volumes of profitable products from the company. Others may be bought largely by customers who buy nothing else from the firm.

The great bulk of the items move in acceptable volume at what the executives consider profitable levels.

In the first four instances, the firm has both a product and a price problem to consider. Those low-profit items being bought by customers who buy little else from him probably do not belong in the assortment at all; they are not items desired by his market segment. Those low-profit items that are not significant to the cost structure of customers in his segment may be candidates for price increases, but he must be sure of the customer attitude. If the price footballs and the price barometer items are needed by his market segment as part of their assortment, then he should probably follow an aggressively low price policy with them, treating them as part of his sales promotion.

THE DISTRIBUTIVE DISCOUNT STRUCTURE

Few products have just one price in the transaction from the maker to the buyer. Most have prices at several levels as they move from factory to wholesaler, perhaps to a subwholesaler, to a retailer, and finally to the ultimate buyer. Even industrial goods frequently pass through at least one extra set of hands before reaching the ultimate buyer. Each unit in the chain of distribution must have some operating margin between the price he pays and the price he sells at, and this discount structure is normally set up originally by the manufacturer and, if well designed for the selling job needed, adhered to by the various elements in the distributive chain. Calculation of such a discount structure usually starts with the final price to the ultimate buyer, aiming for one that will yield the optimum sales volume, and is then figured back, level-by-level, taking account of established trade practice and also what margin is needed to buy from the distributor the kind of sales promotion effort needed without paying for more than will be forthcoming.

In setting up his discount structure, the manufacturer is really a buyer of distribution services needed to make his total product package complete. He has the wide latitude in price offer open to the buyer generally and, like any wise buyer, he must carefully consider whether he is likely to get value received for a higher price. This is not a decision he can make once-and-for-all and then forget it. The margins needed to get the sales promotion element his product package needs change over time, as the need for that sales promotion element changes.

Margins must be high to get the intensive educational and selling effort necessary to acquaint prospects with revolutionary new products, achieve the understanding of the benefits involved that justify changing an established consumption system, and overcome ordinary massive inertia to change. Such margins must be high enough to permit intensive personal selling, if this is possible, or to obtain prominent point-of-purchase advertising display and retail advertising essential to backstopping heavy direct-to-the consumer advertising. Without such intense selling effort all along the line, the final prospect is not likely ever to perceive in the product the potential value for him.

Once the consumer has changed his consumption system so that the product is now an established part of the culture, however, the original long margins purchase less and less, and eventually become an open invitation to retail price discounting as perceptive retailers find volume increases and total profits are more sensitive to price reduction than to selling effort. If margins are not now lowered, they bring on such discounting, engendering distributive chaos and ill will. The history of all major home appliances is a good example. When first introduced, they could be sold only by a door-to-door effort, pressuring the housewife to try them on almost any terms. With the mechanical refrigerator, this process continued nearly to the end of the 1930's. With the end of World War II, however, it took no effort to sell refrigerators, washing machines, and electric ranges, but the retail margins quoted were still the same as when a store had to send out a crew of specialty salesmen. When regular appliance dealers held to old high margins, new "discount" merchants moved in, cutting margins drastically and proving by their volume that demand had become highly price elastic.

The targeted market segment will also determine in part the amount of sales promotion needed in the product package. A good lipstick can be, and is, made to sell for twenty-five cents. But a far larger volume sells for one to several dollars to a different market segment. The cheaper stick sells over the counter in a variety store, probably to relatively rational buyers looking only for a suitable color, consistency, and perfume. The more expensive sticks sell to those who need the assurance of the "cosmetician" behind the department store or drug store counter as to the magical glamor-creating power of the exact stick she is purchasing.

The Psychological Aspects of Price

The buyer has far more freedom in the matter of price than does the seller, for the latter must operate within quite narrow limits determined by rather complex psychological reactions to price.

The precisionist price theorist likes to draw smooth, continuous demand curves to represent the customer's side of price and, so far as monetary systems are concerned, the subdivision of monetary units is so small that this is no very significant approximation. But while the *expression* of price can be represented in such continuous objective form, the actual *psychological operation* of price from the buyer's point of view is in no sense continuous and, in many cases, appears to have a direction opposite to that of the numbers involved. Anyone with experience with real price experimentation and market reaction soon discovers at least four types of psychological reactions to price figures:

1. quantum effects
2. reverse direction perception
3. fair price comparisons
4. cost price standards.

QUANTUM EFFECTS

The newly developed lasers and masers are based on a principle long known to physics: Under certain conditions, the effect of light energy is not continuous, but sometimes has to build up to a certain point to work, then causes a disproportionate end result. A parallel price effect phenomenon is familiar to every supermarket operator. A given product may not move at $1.05, but a package containing only four-fifths as much, clearly labelled as to quantity, will readily sell at 98 cents. One dollar is a quantum point as far as its customers are concerned.

The author had a ringside seat in some practical price experiments demonstrating this quantum effect quite clearly. The firm had just introduced a consumer specialty in three sizes of packages: 5-pound, 10-pound, and 25-pound. The market seemed to require all three sizes, and a somewhat lower quality competing product was packaged in all three sizes, plus a fifty pound size. For this new firm, the economics of packaging cost made the larger size actually more expensive to produce per pound than the two smaller sizes, but the customer expected, of course, to buy it for less per pound. Initially, the suggested retail prices were $.69 for the 5-pound, $1.29 for the 10-pound, and $2.65 for the 25-pound size.

Prices and quality seemed attractive to the market, and all three sizes moved well in the retail outlets. But the seller's margin was so thin on the 25-pound size that the president of the firm decided he could not live with this price structure and so had the retail price of the 25-pound size raised to $2.75. Discovering no drop-off in sales at this level, he then raised it to $2.85, then to $2.95. There was still no visible effect on the retail volume.

Deciding the customer would buy the 25-pound size so long as it was cheaper per pound than the smaller sizes, the official issued a retail price of $3.09. This was still a bargain, relative to the 10-pound size, the price of the latter being equivalent to $3.23 for 25 pounds. But the consumers apparently did not see it this way. Sales of the 25-pound size stopped altogether. Three dollars had proved to be a quantum point.

REVERSE DIRECTION PRICE PERCEPTION

Those who sell clothes say that at certain prices consumers will buy more than at some lower prices. A $2.95 price, for example, may seem to look cheaper to the buyers than a $2.45 price, a 29 cent price may look like less than 24 cents. Thus a price that is higher on the numerical scale proves to be lower on the consumer's psychological scale.

FAIR PRICE STANDARDS

The hump-backed demand curve is not found in the economic texts, but is often encountered in the marketplace. Magazine publishers make frequent tests of subscription prices through mailed special offers, and we are told they frequently find a best price point that will actually secure more subscribers than a point below or above it. In the case of one well-known weekly, this caused them to raise the price by a full third in a recent year.

A major national retail chain ran into this phenomenon with respect to a common hardware item originally priced at $1.19. Concluding the sales were not as good as hoped, they decided on a price experiment, choosing three groups of outlets for experiments. In one group, the item was priced at $.89, in another at $1.09, in the third at $1.29. The stores selling the item at $1.09 moved far greater quantities than those listing it at either $.89 or $1.29, or than had moved at $1.19. Consumers obviously felt that $1.09 was the right price for this item. Probably they considered the $.89 price too low to be a quality item, the $1.19 or higher too much for the item.

Consumers apparently attempt to develop some idea of fair price for many items, even unfamiliar ones. One firm introduced an entirely new type of garden product on the suburban market— a soil-mellowing agent that was permanent in its effect and had no close substitutes. The effect was not chemical, in fact, the mechanism was not clearly understood, but was quite real. The product was quite bulky; the basic package was four cubic feet. Stores stocked it in the fertilizer department. For the home gardener, and indeed for some intensive types of commercial operations, any plausible price that might have been charged would be reasonable in relation to the benefits. But the very bulkiness of the product limited distribution because of high shipping costs. After some carefully observed price trials, it became apparent consumers would pay up to and including the price of a standard sack of mixed fertilizer, but not many would pay more. Whenever the fertilizer price increased, the price of the mellower could be raised along with it. Yet the product was in no sense a fertilizer and was clearly labeled and packaged in a way to distinguish it from the fertilizers. Apparently customers felt that the fair price of this product was the same as that of the fertilizers because it came in a sack and was sold in the same department.

COST PRICE STANDARDS

Whenever the buyer thinks he can judge the cost of production, his fair price standard is a relatively simple one, it must be high enough to allow a modest profit, but no more. Manufacturers of farm equipment, for example, have found that farmers are sufficiently sophisticated mechanically to form judgments on the cost of producing some of the simpler attachments on their machines. As already indicated, the experience of one tractor manufacturer led him to conclude he could not charge more than 25 dollars for the power steering on his tractor even though competitors were getting as much as $200 for the power steering on their machines. Because of his tractor design, his attachment was so simple farmers would conclude the attachment was not worth more, although fully as rugged and effective as the more expensive attachments.

All such fair price concepts may have a rational rationale in a mass production industrial economy in which the seller must count on repeat business for his profit and the buyer is dependent on outside sellers for most of his existence.

The Dynamic and Tactical Aspects of Pricing Decision

Many price decisions are really, on the one side, passive responses to cost squeezes and, on the other, estimated adaptations to what seem to be competitive requirements of the market. Profitable use of price tactics requires a more positive approach than this. Many kinds of price tactics are available to and frequently used by industry. Familiarity with the dynamics of price and price changes is important to the proper use of these tactics. Six kinds of tactical price moves are widely used:

1. the temporary direct or indirect reduction of price
2. promotional pricing
3. price maintenance
4. price followership and leadership
5. incremental pricing
6. off-season pricing.

Every one of these can be a useful tool in some circumstances in expanding or holding profitable markets. But when used without a clear picture of the economic forces and social attitudes involved, each one can cost a company profits.

TEMPORARY PRICE REDUCTIONS

The temporary reduction is a common tactic in industries characterized by uniform or nearly uniform industry prices. It is sometimes used as a temporary defensive maneuver to gain time to counter a successful product move by a competitor. In such cases, it is simple recognition of a discount in consumer value caused by the product move.

The most important use of the temporary reduction is to stimulate sampling by possible new customers who are not acquainted with the product but who can be expected to consider it a preferential product package if they do become familiar with it, in order to extend the market segment covered. If no substantial added potential exists, or if the manner in which the "deal" is planned and executed does not reach this market, the move is self-defeating, cutting into company profits without any offsetting long-run benefits.

The reduction may be in the form of a straightforward temporary reduction in actual price, such as the "8¢ OFF" label on a package of detergent, or a cash refund to anyone mailing in the coupon with a label from a can of Chun-King Chow Mein. Or it may be some other form of "deal," such as a combination of a can of the new aerosol shave lotion, a pack of blades, and a razor for much less than the combined separate prices of all three. If such temporary prices are not to touch off a chaotic price war, they must be clearly labeled as temporary. If they are not to create some sort of reverse value perception on the part of the consumer making him think the lower price means an inferior product, they must be really temporary in execution.

PROMOTIONAL PRICING

Henry Ford was probably one of the first users of promotional pricing on a major scale when, after the end of World War I, a number of successive and substantial price reductions were made for the Model T in order to broaden the market and thereby achieve production economies that would justify the lower prices. Aggressive managements use promotional pricing to break out of a vicious circle in which a product could have wider use if sold for less, and could be produced and sold for less if only it had wider use.

Typically a promotional price is set at a level below current cost, in the expectation that a wide enough potential market will be brought into actuality to create a volume that will in turn bring about a possible cost breakthrough. To be able to get continuous production on what was then a batch rolling process, the aluminum industry, with some success, used this approach with a number of sheet products to raid a number of markets that had been the monopoly of steel.

Such a move obviously requires an accurate estimate of the potential the price cut can add, and of the relative production costs before and after such a volume increase. The move can easily touch off an intra-industry or even inter-industry price battle if the industry whose markets are being raided is well organized and alert to the danger. Retaliation may be in the form of matching price cuts, product improvements, or both.

Dupont precipitated just such a price battle when it decided to concentrate on getting nylon tire cord into original equipment tires and closed out its own rayon cord production. Other rayon producers retaliated with both price cuts and a hard-hitting competitive advertising campaign under a new common label, Tyrex, and thus saved their market for the time being.

New Product Pricing. There is often little choice but to use some kind of promotional pricing for really new products. Any attempt to recover full production costs immediately, on the basis of initial low volume, may well doom the product before it gets off the ground. With the merely improved evolutionary product, on the other hand, a small core market segment may be willing to pay an initial high price giving an early profit. In this case, the firm should nevertheless consider whether the safest long-run policy is such a cream-skimming one, or promotional pricing from the outset to build an entrenched position in a volume market immediately before competition can move in.

Skimming the cream by charging a price equal to the valuation of the initial core market segment can make the profit potential so attractive as to create substantial early competition. However, there may be occasions when the initial high price creates a higher long-run value image, causing late adopters to perceive more value in the product than they would have otherwise. The ease with which competitors can get into production and, in a cream-skimming operation, the wise timing of planned price reductions, which should be carefully programmed in advance, will govern the choice. The degree of emotional content in consumer price evaluation will also be a factor.

Whatever the initial price policy, it will need constant review over the maturing phases of the life cycle. This is especially true of the distributive margins. As already pointed out, the discount structure in particular must be carefully checked to determine the need for revision as the product becomes established.

INCREMENTAL PRICING

Any product has different value to different market segments because some of the product's attributes are considered of little or no value by some market segments. If some of the lower evaluation segments are sealed off from the normal segments, and especially if the undesired attributes can be omitted for the fringe segments, unused production facilities can sometimes be activated to sell to this market segment at a price that covers variable costs and part of overhead. This contribution to overhead can be a real source of additional profit. Thus a shoe factory may take on an order of army specification shoes, without its brand label attribute, at a price that is less than full cost, if it has idle facilities and variable costs are more than covered. The cannery may produce canned peaches for a food wholesaler or chain under the buyer's brand label at a lower price than it would under its own well-advertised label, knowing that the buyers of the private label do not constitute part of the market segment buying his advertised brand. The major brand gasoline refinery may supply the independent lower-priced station with products blended to essentially the same specifications as its own.

Such incremental contributions to overhead, and thus to profit, are real so long as the seller is careful that the segment he serves does not come out of his normal market. This dictates that the total service package be different in aspects important to his core segment, e.g., having a different label, a different channel of distribution, and/or different minor physical attributes. A well-known maker of shotguns, for example, was long the supplier of a very similar firearm to one of the major mail-order companies, under the mail-order company's own brand, selling at a substantially lower price. Besides the different brand name, the barrel had a somewhat duller finish.

OFF-SEASON AND SPECIAL GROUP PRICES

Transportation firms and resort businesses have long recognized that the product and service package being sold during the slack season, and those to special charter and excursion groups, are really different from their regular product, and usually, but not always, tap a different market segment.

Even off-season business that is promoted at the partial expense of the regular season can lower average costs to more than justify price cuts. Mail-order firms have long used special catalog mailings and special offseason offerings to their regular customers to level out their work load over the year. Recently, farm machinery manufacturers have found the off-season price reduction useful, selling machinery during winter months with no payment until later, and even, in some cases, at a sizeable price discount. Besides the internal savings realized, this tactic may also raid some of a competitor's market share if the firm is the first to use it.

PRICE LEADERSHIP AND PRICE FOLLOWERSHIP

In industries in which prices must be identical because of the lack of major product differentiation and the sellers are relatively few, some one member must be first in initiating a price change. Frequently, it is the same one, one of the dominant firms. This price leader bears the responsibility of correctly estimating the market forces. His cuts must not be so drastic that they trigger the vicious circle of a price war. More important, he must be careful not to raise prices to a level that will either attract additional competitors with the same physical product, or make room for competition of other physical products capable of filling some of the service needs of some of the segments served.

The price leader must thus seek to approximate the price that would be an equilibrium price under the current conditions of potential and actual competition. Since this competitive structure is undergoing constant flux, he has a difficult balancing act.

Price leaders, to their sorrow and that of their industry, do not always so act. From the end of World War II until the late 1950's, the steel industry followed a price leadership that focussed so intently on improving the return on old style investment that it was blind to the potential profit it was offering competing materials. The competition was not blind, and plastics, aluminum, prestressed concrete, and even paper took over painfully large chunks of the more profitable markets. Major gasoline marketers in many parts of the country have seemed to try to stabilize prices at levels that would protect an overextended dealer network. Aggressive independents have thus moved in with ease in many markets with lower-cost operations, capturing from one-third to nearly half the gallonage in important centers.

By contrast, Sohio, the acknowledged price leader in Ohio, early learned the bitter fruits of trying to hold an umbrella over too high prices. In the last generation the company has learned to price in relationship to supplies available and market conditions in each area in its territory. As a result, independents have had less lush profits than elsewhere, and their market penetration, even during recent periods of extreme refinery overproduction, has been far less than in any other major consuming area, especially those as well situated as Ohio is to major open market outside supplies.

PRICE MAINTENANCE

No cause is closer to the heart of the *established* seller, especially the small merchant, than maintaining a floor under prices. Since Henry Ford's Model T destroyed his locational monopoly, no session of Congress has been free of pressure from organized merchant lobbies seeking agreements to restrain the trade of those who cut price margins. "Fair trade" is their symbol.

That fair trade legislation has never proved effective in stemming aggressive new competitors has not daunted the persistence of price-fixing advocates, nor has the uniform failure of all sincere efforts by manufacturers to enforce high retail margins while pursuing the intensive distribution policies that make their goods available to any retailer. In their moral indignation at competitors who dare to compete, such merchants ignore the inherent economic impossibility of maintaining a high margin price by fiat once products pass out of the specialty class with selective distribution.

Once a product becomes an established part of the consumption pattern and achieves distribution in nearly every relevant outlet, no amount of legal legerdemain is powerful enough to counter the strong incentive for alert merchants selling well-accepted popular brands to discount price, directly or indirectly, if the number of merchants handling the product in his market area is large. In such a situation, the individual merchant faces a nearly flat demand curve, one of extremely high elasticity, as illustrated in Figure 5-1 (page 140). Any perceptive merchant in such a situation soon realizes that a slight drop in price brings a disproportionate increase in sales volume and a greater total profit (the area $PP'CC'$) if suggested margins are wide. Even when legal harassment prevents direct cuts in price temporarily, he can and does find some way of taking advantage of the excess fat in the price,

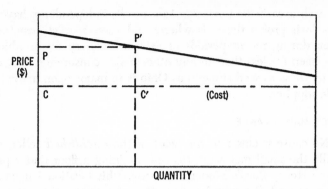

FIGURE 5-1. The Highly Elastic Demand Curve

by adding other services to the product in some way, by utilizing the revenue from the price-fixed item to support deep-cut prices on other products as traffic builders, or by some other device.

There is a way to achieve price stability without legislation, and legally, when needed, and there are circumstances in which high margins are needed and need protection: The introduction of really new products the sale of which must be pioneered by means of intensive personal sales push and various kinds of sales promotion such as heavy and prominent display backed up by both local and market-wide advertising. That method is the simple one of selective distribution, of limiting dealerships to those with the resources and skills to do the kind of job needed and of giving them the incentive by limiting their competition in the immediate vicinity.

In such circumstances, neither the public interest nor that of the manufacturer is served by price cutting competition during the period the product is gaining the acceptance it needs, or for any product requiring the aura of exclusiveness as part of its psychological value. One of the factors that unquestionably doomed the first introduction of the Lincoln Continental (Mark II) after World War II was the tendency of weak dealers to cut price substantially to retrieve their inventory cost. He who buys a $10,000 car is not looking for a price bargain. Ford had made the mistake of abandoning the original sound policy of appointing a few selected strong dealers, none of them in effective competition with each other, and franchised the Continental to almost any Mercury dealer who thought he wanted to handle it.

Selective distribution can effectively maintain dealer margins justified by market needs and is the only way such price margins can be maintained for any length of time. Such dealers are not faced with the elastic demand curve of intensive distribution but with the much less elastic overall demand curve of the overall market for the product; they cannot take sales from each other. Such a policy, however, does not put the product into the weak hands of those most insistent on fair trade protection.

Price as Primarily Incentive

Product is the seller's contribution to the market place, to be exchanged for price, which the buyer brings. As a buyer, the firm has much wider discretion in the price decision than it does as seller. Indeed, many of its price decisions are really buying decisions. It has already been pointed out that the discount structure is really a means of purchasing distributive services needed to complete the product package desired by buyers. Positive use of the buying price can be an important element in profit management.

An office equipment and supply firm, for example, decided that its profit margins on sales were too thin because of the system used in compensating salesmen. They simply changed the base for the bonus and salary from total sales to total gross margin. Total sales went down, but total profit went up. Paying for total sales stimulated the salesman to produce the big orders on which bidding was quite competitive. Paying for total gross margin stimulated the production of orders from smaller buyers who did not have so much competition for their business. The product desired in this case was, of course, a specific kind of sales effort. The same thing can be done with physical goods. Vendor rating systems coming into use by procurement executives are a system of paying for desired vendor performance by means of one kind of price—greater share of business.

Price is the way of leading producers to develop the product packages desired. Whether the buyer is the middle income book-keeper or his big business employer, when he offers enough price, the market sooner or later responds, whether the desired product package is a bechromed Detroit monstrosity or highly uniform raw materials that make production less expensive. It is only necessary to put a profitable premium on the desired product attribute.

Two Special Aspects of Pricing

PRICE CONTROL

The small merchant is not the only one who often thinks there ought to be a law about prices. In the case of buyers, every period of rising prices brings cries for price control, meaning maximum price ceilings, even from the otherwise well-educated. The buyer is just as mistaken about the economic possibility of his desires as is the merchant hungry for fair trade. He wants a limitation on prices without limitation on his spending. But prices can be truly controlled only by drastically limiting the purchasing power that can be applied to the product. Practically speaking, this is always done by issuing a special auxiliary monetary system called *rationing* for consumer goods and *allocation* for industry. No purchases may be made at any price without the auxiliary money in the right amount. We thus sterilize part of the ordinary monetary supply.

But such rationing implies that the amount of every major item of production manufactured is predetermined; consumer freedom of choice cannot be permitted. This, in turn, necessarily implies that the economy is directed to some central purpose. When the nation is in a war for its survival, there is such a purpose on which the overwhelming majority can agree. But when else?

Even so, the degree of effective price control that can be or ever has been achieved even under all-out war conditions can easily be overrated. At best, all that can be held constant is the price quotation for carefully defined physical products. Nothing can be done to hold constant the total service package sold. Some of the service elements of real importance to the buyer will inevitably be restricted or eliminated. Assortments of styles, for example, are certain to be a casualty, and in wartime this is probably to the good. If the product is not a highly standardized one with competing substitutes homogeneous, quality can and does suffer. While industrial goods sold to a limited few can be easily allocated, consumer product allocation is inevitably somewhat uneven, changing consumption patterns in many unpleasant ways and putting a severe strain on the voluntary compliance without which the system cannot work. The steel needed to fill an order for rifles is easily figured from a bill of materials. But the amount of coffee each person should be allowed is not such a definitive amount. I drink none at all, but my wife gulps down three times the per capita average. I can give her my ration ticket, which is fortunate for her, but she is still short one-third her normal usage. The number of consumer commodities is so large, the service package tastes so varied, that the blocked currencies we call ration tickets become too complicated for fair administration.

In fact, there is really only one effective method for consumer rationing, and even no wartime legislator has been brave enough to propose it: direct rationing of the total amount of money that can be spent, alleviated somewhat by what might be called a limited government black market in spending tokens at high prices, for those whose money burns holes in their pockets.

One additional fact of political life is usually disregarded: no governmental agency can be as harsh on the inefficient as the market itself. Ceilings will never be set that will deliberately put the marginal business out of action. In peacetime, price ceilings by legal fiat are just as much a chimera as effective price floors; they disregard the economic incentives they set in action.

CONSUMER CREDIT PRICES

This generation is so used to consumer credit for everything from Bermuda vacations to automobiles and the baby's wardrobe that we tend to forget that such widespread use is less than two generations old. The price reactions of those market segments who depend on it are quite different from the price behavior of those who buy mainly for cash. The credit seller who mentions only the size of the periodic payment, not the price, is on the right track. This is the only information the regular credit buyer is concerned with.

For the regular credit buyer, price is the weekly payment, not the final cumulative total. Thus a lengthening of the payment period acts the same in the affected markets as a price decrease, its shortening the same as a price increase. The tremendous burst of automobile sales in the middle 1950's was induced by just such a lengthening of the period of payment for automobile loans.

Such a change in credit terms does more than simply increase total sales quantities, however. It temporarily distorts the price-line mix itself. Buick became, for a time, the third most popular make, ranking right after Ford and Chevrolet, and other middle-range makes benefitted proportionately. This caused the auto industry to assume a permanent shift in buying habits had taken place and induced expansion of facilities for such makes, including the decision to launch the ill-starred Edsel. Later markets demonstrated the temporary nature of this credit-inspired upgrading of buying habits.

Summary

1. Price is a day-to-day tactical tool of competition and one in which the latitude of decision to the seller is highly restricted by the nature of product, industry patterns, and buyer attitudes.

2. In some industries, prices must be uniform as between sellers. Such uniform price situations are of two types. In one, there are traditional prices which cannot be broached. A candy bar always sells for a nickel or a dime. Usually, however, price variation does take place, in terms of quantity variation in the content. Even so, sizes must be comparable at any given time, regardless of relative quality. In other industries, prices may shift their level from time to time, but in unison. In both cases, the successful seller is rewarded by a larger share of market and lower cost in getting it, giving him a form of margin elasticity.

3. Prices are set to yield some target return on investment, or on sales, or to break-even on the basis of a minimum sales estimate in industries in which products differ so much from possible competing substitutes that no useful guides to the market are

available. Return-on-investment is used as a guide, in combination with costs estimated on standard volume, in highly cyclical industries. In the latter case, care must be taken to consider the possible attraction being given to latent competition.

4. In other industries, prices are divided into a number of price lines. In such an event, the only price choice open is for which price lines the seller can best engineer product to meet cost and quality specifications.

5. Truly differentiated prices are characteristic of complex products for which differentiation is multidirectional. Quite often the buyer judges price, not on the total package he selects (and he usually has options), but on the quotation on some component. The problem becomes one of determining the basis of the customer's comparisons with substitute product packages.

6. Competitive bid prices are based on a combination of the hunger of the bidder for the contract, his estimate of the probable bids of competitors, and his judgment as to the special advantages any bidder has in securing the contract. A technique known as competitive bidding strategy can help him make a more accurate appraisal of the profitability to him of any given bid, based on past performance of each competitor.

7. Most pricing decisions deal not with a single price, but with the structure of prices between items in a product line, whether of the complementary type or of the mutually exclusive choice type, and with the structure of discounts in a channel of distribution. In pricing a product in the complementary product line, the line is really the product, and the relative prices are intended to make the assortment as a whole attractive. In the mutually exclusive case, target pricing is common, with the average profit yield the target, and some prices set to make attractive comparison with near-substitute products. The discount structure decision is really a buying decision, using the discount as an incentive to call forth whatever level of distributive effort is required.

8. Buyer reaction to price has psychological aspects not obvious from the numbers used to express price. Very common types of reactions are quantum effects, reverse direction perception, fair price comparisons, and cost price standards.

9. Pricing can be used as an aggressive tactical tool. The principal tactical moves are: temporary direct or indirect reductions, promotional pricing, price maintenance, price followership and leadership, incremental pricing, and off-season pricing.

10. In times of rising prices, consumers have a tendency to talk about price control. They do not realize this cannot be done without restricting their purchasing power through a complex and cumbersome form of money we call rationing.

11. Consumer credit sales price reactions are a phenomenon in themselves. Price is judged solely on the basis of the periodic payment, making changes in credit terms equivalent to changes in prices.

6

Determination of
Economic Cost

Cost Is Relative to the Decision

As the selling-below-cost laws in a number of states imply, most people, including lawmakers, consider cost a very definitive figure. In actuality, few economic concepts have a more slippery content. The cost of an item can only be determined after we know the purpose for which we propose to use the cost calculation. The accuracy of this calculation will depend on whether we are concerned merely with the historical record or intend to use it to estimate the costs involved in a decision alternative.

Even when cost is being used to appraise past performance, expenditures that should be included will vary according to the degree of *accountability* of the individual, department, or economic unit being judged. If the unit be the entire firm, in its report to stockholders, the only problem may be to separate capital expenditures, whose costs should properly be spread over the longer-run benefit period, from the true current costs. (Even in this area, expert accountants disagree on the proper practice. Since this disagreement does not concern the kinds of profit comparisons management makes about possible alternative investments, however, it is of no concern in this discussion.)

On the other hand, when a single department of a business is being judged, the evaluation must omit costs beyond the control of that department. Thus, if a department is arbitrarily charged with materials bought from another department with no choice as to source, it cannot be held accountable for cost variations due to acceptance of these materials. Neither can it be held accountable for any allocation of the general company overhead. Thus we find reference in management literature to *controllable* and *uncontrollable costs.* Such distinctions are primarily a subject of personnel and organizational management and control, however, not of economic decision.

The economic decision commonly concerns itself with the use of past costs as a major basis for the estimation of probable future costs. The length of time to be covered by the effect of the decision then becomes the major determinant as to which expenditures are cost and which not relevant to the decision, and those costs will include both actual expenditures and unseen ones. Consider the case of a firm considering the construction of a plant to make a new product. There are visible elements of cost in every item connected with the planning, construction, and eventual utilization of this plant and the marketing operation involved, and all of them should be counted in the total cost. But the total must also include other elements of real economic cost that will not appear on the books of account.

Adoption of this project means forgoing alternate opportunities for profit through use of the funds appropriated for its realization. Its prosecution will preempt some resources already on hand such as land, buildings, equipment, and organization talent. Some of these real costs will not show in the accountant's figures. They are hidden, or imputed costs, and we must add into the estimate some sacrifices of income or opportunity involved in this decision and perhaps subtract some imputed losses that would be incurred by failure to proceed.

For such costs of *not doing* can be either positive or negative. Failure to introduce a new product may jeopardize the market position of the company and adversely affect profits. The estimated profit loss would be a cost subtraction for such a long-term project.

At the other extreme are such short-term decisions as one to make a one-time sale of some standard product of ours to a market to which we do not normally have access and which does not overlap some of our other market segments and, in so doing, utilize idle resources such as idle plant capacity and labor or otherwise worthless by-product materials. For such an extreme short-run decision, the only relevant costs are those actual cash outlays that would be added by going ahead with the filling of this one order such as cost of added raw materials that would not otherwise be bought and cost of such labor as would not otherwise be on the payroll. Any revenue obtained over and above these directly attributable added expenses is a contribution to overhead and thus to eventual profit. The by-product raw material used may be costless if it has no alternative use. Labor force that would otherwise have been kept on at any kind of task just to hold it intact is also costless even though the books show wages actually paid out.

In other words, in any decision involving only such short-run considerations as this one, the only relevant costs are those that are *incremental,* those incurred as a direct result of the decision that would not otherwise have to be met.

The two simplified illustrations above highlight some of the more important relationships between decision needs and cost allocation. They involve most of the concepts used in discussing economic cost. Let us consider some of these concepts.

Outlay versus Alternative Opportunity Costs

Books of account usually carry only those costs resulting from actual cash outlays and include all such costs without regard to those directly attributable to this one decision. But many decisions involve real costs that do not show up as any kind of cash transaction, and some of the actual cash outlays incurred are not true economic costs, relative to that decision.

Depreciation reserves a firm has may be used in undertaking an expansion, for example. This money, although on hand and not borrowed, has a real cost. It costs whatever return it could bring in the next best alternate use. Or we could charge its use with the interest the firm would have to pay to borrow the money—the alternative source of funds. In deciding to use the funds on hand for this expansion, the firm is sacrificing—spending, in other words —income it would otherwise receive from this money in some other profit venture, or saving the cost of the borrowing for this purpose (and probably incurring an interest cost for some other purpose).

Similarly, the new plant may occupy land bought many years before, at a price much lower than it could now be sold for. The cost of the land for this project is no longer the original cost, but the cost the land would bring if put on the market. If it did not already own the property, it would have to buy it at the current market price. The latter is the real cost, even though the books may show a different figure.

Labor that would be kept on in any event to hold a skilled workforce intact obviously results in a cash payroll outlay. But this outlay is no part of the real cost of a job taken on simply to keep the force busy. Nor can any of the plant overhead outlays be charged against such a job. They would go on without reference to the decision to take or reject such an order. Only the difference in cost between doing and *not doing* is an economic cost.

Most cost decisions are between the extremes of long-run and short-run. Regardless of the length of time affected, the true economic cost and the real economic profit of a decision are measured in relation to the *opportunity costs* involved. Good opportunity cost estimates require care in uncovering all of the available facts determining the alternate opportunities (one of which is always the opportunity of *not doing*). The last illustration was carefully limited to a one-time order from a market to which the firm did not normally have access, and which did not overlap its normal market segment, i.e., a completely sealed-off market segment. Such completely sealed-off segments are rare; some overlap is more common. If an overlap is present, consideration of the relative losses and the effect on the rest of the marketing operation would have to enter into cost estimates and be judged in comparison with the alternate costs involved.

Whatever the basis, all costs must be evaluated with regard to the decision's effects on the entire system involved in the firm's operations—its full marketing operation as well as the entire production operation. It may be profitable to assume added costs in production if this is offset by greater savings in shipping costs, materials purchasing, handling costs, marketing expense, or costs in any other part of the operation. Costs far outside the sphere ordinarily considered parts of production are real costs of any production decision.

Escapable, Unavoidable, Shutdown, and Standby Costs

When we use the term *incremental costs,* we usually imply increases in the firm's activity. But contraction has also to be faced at times. The same logic determines which costs are relevant as when the decision concerns activity changes in the positive direction, except that we now refer to *escapable* or *unavoidable* costs.

Hence, at the end of 1963, when the Studebaker board of directors learned that the automobile end of the business was continuing to lose money on the basis of the best accounting information, they had to go beyond these accounting calculations. Losses now had to be recalculated to determine which of the figures were mere accounting conventions and which costs the company could hope to escape if it ceased making automobiles. The problem was to estimate which alternative form of reduced activity carried the lowest cost of *not doing.* For an operating plant, labor cost was a true variable in the sense that a cut in the force brought a proportionate cut in cost. But a complete shutdown involved a real added outlay—severance pay. Production equipment of real value to a going plant and of real sales value when sold one piece at a time, might have a much lesser value in terms of complete plant liquidation. Had it been decided to close down only part of the operation and hold the plant involved as a standby for some other purpose, certain *standby costs* would have been required, e.g., watchmen, equipment maintenance, and water service. The correct standard, again, is the cost of the alternate opportunities open—complete shutdown, or various levels of partial suspension—in contrast to trying to continue.

Urgent versus Postponable Costs

Sometimes it may seem that revenues and even sources of borrowed funds are so limited that all costs not absolutely necessary to keep the firm in business must be eliminated or postponed. Costs then tend to be grouped into those which are *urgent* and those which are *postponable.*

Certain of the costs may appear temporarily at the discretion of management without many obvious unacceptable immediate effects. These are *discretionary expenditures.* Thus research and development funds and advertising appropriations may be cut and postponed at management discretion without effect on the revenues for the current year. Proper costing of such changes in discretionary expenditures must include the best possible estimate of the hidden costs of such cuts. Cutting its research and development expense in half may reduce the company's outgo by a half million dollars, for example. But the end cost may be 10 million dollars in profit if a less economy-minded competitor pushes ahead regardless of cash stringency and grabs a share of the firm's market segment with his own improved product. The inertia of the market is such that advertising and selling expense cuts seldom have an immediately visible effect, even when the cuts are deep. But the momentum sacrificed may enable some competitor or some competing type of product to gain a foothold otherwise denied him. In both cases, the net cost of the reduction would be far higher than the immediate reduction in outgo. Such outlay reductions are in no sense the equivalent of economic cost savings.

Estimate of the possible losses is hard, of course, and never will be precise. But the costs of the opportunities forgone must be estimated when evaluating such cutback alternatives. In a dynamic economy such as ours, ignoring the ultimate cost can prove costly indeed.

Sunk Costs

We call expenditures that have actually been incurred, but which cannot be recovered whichever way a decision goes, *sunk costs.* Consider the example of a cattle feeder who has paid $30 per hundredweight for lean steers he has bought to fatten for market. Suppose that during the time he is feeding them the livestock market declines drastically to $24 per hundredweight, and he decides to cut feeding early and sell in the belief the market will go down further, at least to $22 per hundredweight, if he waits any longer. If his estimate is correct, and the market does drop by another $2, his decision to sell *at that time* earned him a profit of $2 per hundredweight, even though he sustained a real loss on the total operation of $6 per hundredweight, plus the cost of the feed used up. This loss of $6 and the feed is not relevant to the profitability of the decision to sell at this particular time. The money is already paid out and cannot be recovered. All that is relevant is the prospect of future prices, and by selling now, the feeder is $2 per hundredweight ahead of where he will be if he waits. The $30 originally paid, like most past expenditures, is sunk.

Depreciation: Obsolescence and Wear-and-Tear

Part of the depreciation we carry on our books is a form of sunk cost, i.e., that part due to pure time, or obsolescence. When you drive the new family chariot off the showroom floor, it immediately loses value and continues to lose value with each passing day even if you park it in your garage and never move it again. It is being superseded in style and newness by other shiny new models. You can do nothing about this part of depreciation cost—it is sunk.

But other parts of the losses we charge to depreciation may have nothing to do with time. They are incurred by your decision to use the car, to subject it to ordinary wear-and-tear. Some items of wear-and-tear become due quite regularly and we class them as current expenses, e.g., periodic lubrication and purchases of spark plugs. Other use costs occur at relatively infrequent periods and can be treated as semitime charges. The tires, for example, may last over fifty thousand miles if you keep the car that long. Under normal circumstances, you may very well trade in the car before you need either tires or a major engine overhaul. In such a case, the overhaul and new tire costs become part of the depreciation expressed as the difference between original price and trade-in value. But if you were a salesman with a territory requiring a hundred thousand miles of travel per year, both might be charged off to a separate wear-and-tear account. Such wear-and-tear can be an incremental cost.

Direct Cost and Indirect Cost

The accounting profession has recently given some attention to a costing procedure similar to the economist's division of costs into *fixed* and *variable*. It is labeled *direct costing*. In some presentations, there appears to be no difference between the concept of direct cost and the economist's variable cost. The economist will define variable costs as those varying directly with the volume of an item produced, and the accountant will define direct cost, in much the same terms, as costs such as raw materials, direct labor, and direct supplies, plus costs that vary closely with production and can be allocated to it, such as electric power and foremen's wages.

Other writers, however, seem to include in direct costs any that are directly traceable to a given item of production, which could include some costs the economist considers as fixed or even sunk costs. One problem is that the accountant must follow the same rules all of the time in making his cost allocations. What may well be variable cost in terms of one kind of decision may be a fixed cost in terms of another. For example, a decision requiring the doubling of near-capacity production must treat supervisory salaries and warehousing as variable costs. By contrast, a decision, when production is at a low level, to make a modest 5 percent increase, may treat all supervisory and inventory costs as fixed.

Standard Costs

Any firm must consider costs of some sort in any pricing decision, if only using them to decide whether or not it is worthwhile entering the market at the existing price level. But if the industry is one with a relatively volatile demand from year-to-year, prices cannot be raised in years when demand is short simply because costs are up, and low earnings in such years need to be offset with extra earned margins in years when demand is high and average costs down.

As a result, the automobile industry and many others have adopted *standard costing*. Basically, this requires the allocation of fixed costs on an estimate of such costs under the long-run average level of production, combining this fixed-cost allocation with variable costs to give a "standard" cost for a "standard" level of product volume. The price decision is then based on this standard cost, which is seldom the actual cost for any one given year.

Costs in a Multiple Product Situation

The previous discussion has centered around the costing of *a* product. The single product firm is the exception, however, not the rule, and the multiproduct firm has a very real problem in allocating joint costs. Any firm selling more than one product uses some resources and facilities jointly for different products, and such joint costs must be allocated by some rule. Accountants tend to use some arbitrary variable cost to apportion allocated costs, e.g., the amount of direct labor involved, the amount of floor space required, or some combination of similar variable measures.

Such accounting allocations are usually quite arbitrary and should be recognized as such. No base can always take into account all of the possible alternatives involved in different kinds of decisions. A cost that is invariable within the area of the decision sought may be treated as variable under the costing procedure. For example, doubling a product's sales volume by reason of some decision will not necessarily double the sales and administrative costs of handling it. In some instances, total sales cost may actually be lowered and administrative costs not affected at all. No rule-of-thumb costing procedure can substitute for a careful determination of exactly which costs are opportunity costs in relation to any major decision.

Exactly in what direction the opportunity costs lie will depend on the basis for the decision that puts the product into the company's line. From the standpoint of production decision, products can be classified into three types:

1. *Products that must be produced jointly.* The smelter of copper ore must inevitably produce not only copper, but some sulphur dioxide. He can throw this sulphur dioxide away by letting it float into the atmosphere, or he can transform it into sulphuric acid. The refiner of crude petroleum must produce heavy fuel oils and lubricating oils as well as gasoline and kerosene.

2. *Products that can be produced partly or wholly at the expense of each other.* The petroleum refiner we just mentioned can vary the amount of light fuel oils and kerosene produced at the expense of gasoline volume, and vice versa, and his demand for the products varies at different times of the year (fortunately, in a complementary manner).

3. *Products produced relatively independently of each other.* The automobile manufacturer, for example, can produce not only passenger cars, but trucks and even tractors. While some of the same equipment can be used for all three, the decision to produce trucks usually requires addition of new facilities. Market demand, and the skill of the firm in serving it, determines the additions of products to such product lines.

INSEPARABLE JOINT PRODUCTS

Relative market demand and relative price margin obtainable should determine cost allocation for products that must be produced together. If any are true by-product production, the only costs of any sort that can be allocated against them are the added ones necessary to put them into forms desired by customers and to sell them. If the copper smelter decides to go into the sulphuric acid business, the sulphur dioxide obtained from the smelter operation would not be a cost for the acid operation unless the possible profit from the acid were one of the considerations that made the whole operation economically feasible. In the latter case, some of the overhead costs must be assessed against the acid operation, how much depending on the market demand for the acid as compared with the blister copper.

Development of by-product production may even have a negative cost at times. Discard of the by-product materials may be so obnoxious to the surrounding community that some acceptable provision must be made for their disposal or the facility will be outlawed. The cost of moving the facility then becomes one of the decision alternatives, and the gain from not moving becomes a contribution to the cost of transformation of the by-product into a saleable commodity.

JOINT PRODUCTS PRODUCIBLE IN VARIABLE PROPORTIONS

With valuable products that are necessarily joint, but with variable relative quantities (such as gasoline and kerosene), the production decision will not usually hinge on the cost allocation. Instead, the latter will hinge on the relative strength of market demand for the various products, to which production will be attuned. Fixed cost allocation should be a reflection of profit in such cases rather than relative profit a reflection of cost allocation.

PRODUCTS PRODUCED RELATIVELY INDEPENDENTLY

Most multiple product lines have been developed for market reasons rather than production necessity. In such cases, the nature of the market demand that occasioned their inclusion in the line must be a major element in the relative costs. From the market standpoint, such product lines are of four general types:

1. multiple products with a relatively independent market demand, brought together because they contribute to production efficiencies, or for financial reasons such as combined automobile and truck production
2. products that supplement each other such as spare parts along with the total automobile, a service network along with a sales operation, or a number of model types of automobiles
3. products combined into a line because customers desire an assortment of goods and insist on limitation of the number of

sources of supply such as sugar the grocer must carry whether or not it is profitable, the ladies' hosiery the department store must carry, top coats and slacks the men's clothing store must carry as well as suits, or aluminum sheets and shapes the steel warehouse must carry as well as steel items

4. products combined in order to lower the average sales cost per item sold and included in the desired assortment bought by customers such as adding machines and office supplies handled along with typewriters, not because customers require it, but because the same customers will buy them, thus lowering overall sales cost per dollar of volume.

Presumably, in the case of *products with an independent market demand,* some kind of incremental analysis entered into the decision to include each in the line, and the reasoning in back of this inclusion would be the first basis of allocation. Later reappraisals might allocate joint costs on some basis such as the amount of key resources and executive attention required in their successful production and sale.

Supplementary products are really different aspects of the same single product package, as defined in this book, and comparative costs would be irrelevant to business decision.

Items that must be carried in the line because the market demands a limited number of supply sources, the seller cannot choose to drop and thus eliminate costs. The line itself is his product, and his only choice is between the kind and amount of costs he will incur in making it available. If he can choose to get it manufactured outside his own organization, then the cost of the outside purchase is one opportunity cost for an item. If he can produce it for less himself, then he makes a profit even though he may sell the individual item for less than his production cost. On the other hand, if he chooses to make it himself even if he could buy for less, then the sales operation may be properly charged only its possible purchase price. Any additional cost must be charged against whatever purpose led to the decision to make rather than buy (such as the desire to level out a seasonal production cycle).

Traffic-building items included in such a line in order to gain or maintain some important profitable portion of the business are really part of the sales promotion effort for the main profitable items. Cost for such sales-supporting items must be compared not with revenues and profits of the individual items, but with the total revenue and profit brought in with the item compared with that obtainable without it. The grocer may make no money on the sugar he sells, but if he does not always have it in stock, the total traffic in his store will be so much less and the sales of other really profitable items will suffer so much that his total profit will diminish drastically.

In all joint cost problems of this sort, the concept of *contribution to overhead* must be the primary consideration. This is simply the difference between the total added revenues secured with the inclusion of the item, and those costs that could have been avoided by not carrying the item. The allocation of costs to traffic-building items should be a function of the margin obtained, not the reverse. This is, indeed, the practice of every merchant, when he uses a variable margin to determine his price structure, expecting a low margin from those products that will not bear a higher one, and a high margin from other products to offset his major fixed costs.

When *items are carried in order to lower the total percentage of sales cost,* this contribution of each item to overhead and sales and administrative cost is the only relevant cost measure, after allowance for the variable cost of handling and producing each and for directly attributable programmed costs.

Some Special Problems of Cost Determination

Costs are of many kinds. Some of them are *a direct function of production*. They vary with the number of units produced. The amount of raw material used up in making the product and the wages of the men on the assembly line are good examples.

Other costs have a *stairstep formation* and are sometimes called semivariable costs by economists. That is, they are fixed costs over certain ranges of the production level, but must increase abruptly when that production level is exceeded. A production department must have at least one foreman to operate at all, and perhaps only one will be needed to run the department at full tilt on a single shift basis. But if a second shift is added, another foreman must be appointed regardless of the size of the second shift operation.

Some costs probably have some kind of relationship to volume, but the extent is not determinable, and their size is determined by executive decision. Among such *programed costs* would be the size of the advertising budget, frequently a matter of arbitrary decision. The volume of sales the firm gets is related in some manner, presumably, to this appropriation, or at least to some of the appropriations in the past. But the exact relationship is seldom knowable, and the size of the cost is determined by executive fiat. So also, frequently, is the size of the sales force and the costs of supervising, training, and operating that sales force.

Some costs have no direct relationship to production at all as long as the firm operates at all; they are *inescapable*. The rent that must be charged, whether paid directly or imputed to the cost of property owned by the firm, is such an inescapable cost, as is usually the president's salary. As already indicated, that part of the depreciation charge due solely to time and obsolescence is unrelated to production and is also inescapable.

Summary

1. Cost is not a fixed value. The term can have meaning only in relation to the decision purpose for which the cost figure is to be used. As a result, there are a number of ways of classifying costs. In addition, for the purpose of decision, actual past costs, however calculated, serve only as bases for estimation of probable future costs.

2. The most important distinction is between *outlay costs*, representing real cash expenditures as they appear on the books, and *opportunity costs*, representing the actual economic sacrifice attributable to a given decision. Not all cash outlays are economic costs in the sense that the decision made would have affected their incurrence, and not all real economic costs show up on the books as cash outlays (the rent that could be obtained from the

building the firm owns and uses, for example). Which costs, including cash outlays, should be charged against a decision will depend on the opportunity afforded of avoiding them, on the time span involved, and on other considerations.

3. When the decision involves an increase, expansion, or change that is not a decrease in scale, we usually charge off the added or *incremental costs* resulting from that decision, i.e., the added cost of doing as compared with the costs of *not doing*. When special costs are incurred because of a decrease in scale or a complete shutdown, we refer to the added costs incurred as *inescapable, unavoidable, shutdown,* or *standby costs.*

4. Expenditures for activities that can be curtailed because of emergency decisions may be divided into *urgent* and *postponable costs.* When arriving at such a classification, recognition must be given to possible future losses that may far outweigh possible current savings from the reduction in such easily postponed costs as research and development and advertising appropriations.

5. *Sunk costs* are actual past cash outlays the incidence or recovery of which will not be affected by a given decision and therefore are *not costs* for the purpose of that decision.

6. *Direct cost* has recently been added to the accountant's vocabulary. Some seem to use the term synonymously with the economist's *variable cost.* Some seem to mean any cost traceable to the operation, whether or not variable in terms of a proposed decision. In any event, no rigid classification can hope to be used as an all-purpose measure of costs for every kind of decision.

7. *Standard costs* are estimates of what the long-run average equivalent of present cost functions would be. The main use of this calculation is the appraisal of the possible price structure for products whose demand is highly cyclical (such as automobiles), and for which fixed costs are an important part of the whole.

8. Costing is complicated by the fact that most firms make multiple products for which many costs are incurred jointly. Such *joint costs* must be allocated to each of the products on the basis of some kind of formula.

9. Accounting practice generally uses some directly attributable variable cost as an arbitrary basis for allocation of joint costs, e.g., direct labor required or the floor space occupied. Such

arbitrary standards seldom measure correctly the opportunity costs of many of the necessary decisions. The only accurate method is to compare the cost opportunities involved in the reason for the joint production.

10. Some joint products are *joint by necessity*, platinum produced in mining for nickel, for example. If some of the joint products are true by-products in the sense that production would proceed in their absence, then only those incremental costs necessary to rendering the by-products marketable and selling them can be charged to them as cost.

11. In other cases, such as the joint production of gasoline and kerosene, *joint production cannot be avoided, but the proportions can be varied* and will be proportioned to expected demand. In such a case, cost allocation to the individual product is without point. Excess of return over variable costs should simply be credited to joint costs and profit. No decision will hinge on any joint cost allocation.

12. Most joint production is of assortments of items produced together for *convenience and to meet marketing requirements.* The nature of the marketing decision leading to their inclusion in the line should determine the cost allocation. Quite frequently, the allocation should be determined by the relative profit, rather than the reverse.

7

Planning for Capital Investment

THE MOST DIFFICULT expenditure decisions made by management are those the effects of which come in over a long period of time, precisely *because* these effects are spread over a considerable period in the future. The farther ahead we must forecast such capital expenditures and similar obligations (such as long term leases), the less able are we to foresee the size of the actual benefit that may result.

Choosing the best course of action requires careful attention to every one of these six steps:

1. thorough consideration of all possible alternatives
2. the most sophisticated forecasting of the income flows and the outlays implicit in the proposition that can be expected
3. choice of a proper method of computing the cost of the capital involved
4. choice of a realistic method of estimating the worth of the result now for each of the alternative kinds of investments to be considered
5. development of a wise standard for selecting among the alternatives
6. not the least important, a post-audit of previous decisions in order to test the kinds of assumptions that have been made and to perfect the use of these assumptions in the future.

Unfortunately, most previous studies have focussed on the fourth point, the method of estimating the present worth of future investments. The econometricians can develop some rather interesting formulas with the look of great precision in this field, and it makes a fertile field for speculation—if you do not worry about the care with which alternatives have been chosen or the accuracy of the forecasts on which the present worth is based. But any computation of present worth must be based on a forecast of possible benefit resting on incomplete information and can seldom take into account the effect of all the various kinds of feed-backs to be expected as a result of carrying out the decision. It takes more than a precise-looking formula to get a precise answer.

In fact, precision can not be expected from most capital budgeting decisions. Business men are aware that such imprecision exists, although they seldom allow enough leeway for uncertainty. They are, thus, far more likely to use rough-and-ready heuristic rules of thumb such as the payoff period in estimating the value of an investment. These rules of thumb have less theoretical value than the academic solutions usually proposed but often turn out to be useful approximations on close examination. Without question, the greatest errors in management of capital do not come from the kinds of formulas used in computing, but from insufficient consideration of alternatives and from improper assumptions as to the extent and durability of the benefits to be expected. And unless past choices are carefully post-audited to learn where they went right and where they went wrong, future decisions are likely to be as poor as any made in the past.

Making Sure of What the Choices Are

Probably the greatest mistake made in deciding on capital expenditures is to believe that many decisions are really of an either/or variety, e.g., whether or not we should expand the store area or whether we should replace this lathe with one that is proposed. It is seldom true that alternatives are of such a simple dichotomous nature. A need to expand operations may often be an occasion for considering the possibility of expanding in other directions or in other places rather than merely a choice between expanding or not expanding. The need to replace machinery or equipment might easily be an occasion for considering whether or not the entire production process is in need of thorough re-evaluation, or the product design itself, or even whether or not the company should be making the product or marketing it or dropping it entirely.

There is only one rule of any value for finding such alternatives, the rule that management itself must have a fervent attitude of forever searching for possible choices and methods of improvement—an attitude so obvious that it is communicated, if possible, down to the last man on the assembly line. Without such an attitude itself, any mechanisms intended to bring out alternatives will probably fall far short of success. With it, there are various mechanical means for assuring that possibilities come to management's attention. Without question, one of the major differences between the success of the various industrial suggestion systems has lain in the attitude of management itself. Anyone who has ever acquainted himself with the Lincoln Electric Company's operation in Cleveland will be impressed by the fact that the extreme success achieved by this company is due to an almost religious belief in possible improvement on the part of management which has been implemented and carried down to the last worker on the line. Furthermore, as indicated briefly in the discussion on the learning curve, a constant management belief in the possibility of improvement will alert management to the lack of improvement when it should be expected.

Probably the greatest source of carelessness in consideration of alternatives comes from the tendency of the executive to focus primarily on his day-to-day problems. This is a hard focus to avoid; today's problems must be taken care of and tomorrow's are easily postponed. One way to get around this attitude is to separate the functions of planning from those of day-to-day operations and some of this can be done. But it is far more important for management to realize that many of today's problems are there because they were not taken care of yesterday. Often the problem is acute because alternatives were not investigated far enough ahead of time.

The growing bureaucratization of industry because of the growth of both the economy and of large-scale production has probably contributed heavily in many cases to the lack of an imaginative search for new products. Far too often, the man who tries something new, even though it is obviously a more profitable risk, is subject to censure, while he who travels in well worn ruts by choice is rewarded for his lack of initiative. Failure in trying the so-called tried-and-true is seldom punished. For this reason, a small fast-moving entrepreneur, not saddled with a large organization as yet, can often elbow his way in among the company of giants and run away with the ball game. Combatting the bureaucratic tendency of a large organization is not easy. Dupont is said to have a policy of rewarding more heavily the man who undertakes something against the advice of the rest of the organization than one who simply succeeds when he goes along with this advice. But even Dupont has not been uniformly successful in keeping ahead in every one of the fields it is in. Whatever the device used, it should be kept constantly in mind that the obvious choices often do not include the most profitable ones, and a careful search for alternatives is a necessary part of any capital decision.

Forecasting Expected Incomes and Outlays

Uncertainty and the future are two sides of the same coin, and in forecasting the future most people are divided between the two extremes of being too optimistic about opportunities or too blind about their probability. And in both cases the forecast is usually the result of too naive a use of the persistence forecast, the belief that things will continue to be as they are and relationships and advantages will remain as they appear at the present time. This is especially likely in forecasting the differential cost advantage conferred by some particular type of production investment when the benefit to be expected is a cost saving. Generally speaking, management tends to make the assumption that cost structures will remain as they are at the time the decision is being made. There is probably no greater fallacy, especially in those cases where a major change is being made in the production structure. Such changes are bound to change the demand and supply equations on which costs are themselves based. If labor costs are initially reduced, quite often a considerable portion of this cost must be given up to labor itself. Furthermore, if the cost change gives any advantage to the particular firm, other organizations competing with it are bound to have, thereby, a strong incentive to match this change and thus nullify the initial advantage given. It is interesting to note that the Lincoln Electric Company's system of compensating employees for process improvement suggestions assumes that the advantage will be of little value after the first year, that competitors will learn of and make use of whatever is gained. This unusual company keeps ahead simply by always making sure it has additional new advances coming along through their own suggestion system.

The same phenomenon is true in the product field, of course. As the product gets older, it gets less productive of profits. In an industry in which new product ferment is quite strong such as the chemical field, the only way to remain on the high profit side is to keep a constant stream of new products coming along. Again, a well-managed company such as Dupont figures the profitable life of a new chemical plant at a mere four years.

The profit to be expected from a capital investment comes from one or a combination of two sources: (1) reductions in cost or (2) expansion of market opportunities. A typical example of the first would be the replacement of an ordinary lathe or milling machine with a numerical control machine, for example. Such cost control investments typically do more than change the level of cost. They almost inevitably change the *proportion* of the production factors used and quite usually the mixture of fixed and variable costs. Typically also, they tend to make use of an opportunity that is or soon will be available to everyone else in the industry. Thus the premising of profit calculations on historical accounting data can be quite dangerous in this situation. The change in the cost structure may involve quite extensive changes throughout the organization if the major benefits are to be realized, and the end results of these changes are not easily forecast nor are they likely to be simple extensions of the kinds of cost on which historical data is gathered by accountants. In any event, the proper measure is, of course, the incremental or cost changes brought about by proposal, and it is extremely important that every individual cost be reviewed to be sure that it is not an arbitrary allocation but is a true economic cost under the new situation that will be brought about.

Difficult as it may be to forecast the outcome beyond the very near future for cost reduction investments, the forecast is far more complex for investments in plant expansion, extension of a distribution system, the introduction of new products, or the undertaking of a major change in promotional activity designed to build markets. In general, the changes brought about are both in total sales and in the cost structure itself. Where the change involves product, the problem becomes the very difficult one of forecasting the tastes and needs of customers in the future. Where the investment involves major expenditures for promotional purposes, we have practically no means of estimating with any degree of precision the amount of effect being procured by any particular level of dollar expenditure. All such long term investment calculations, moreover, must make some assumptions concerning the future action of competitors, present and potential, that may affect profit.

Two special problems of forecasting the effect of product adoption or change need careful consideration. One is the fit of the product to the assets available for its market development, and the second is the degree to which product fits into current consumption systems. In considering the assets, we need to go far beyond the dollars on the balance sheet. The most important assets to be considered are the personal and organizational abilities within the firm that determine the degree to which the company can attain some kind of differential advantage. The dollars are important also, and how important depends upon the degree to which a product fits the consumption system. If a new product drops readily into the ordinary use patterns of currently available products, the cash flows to be expected back from its introduction can reasonably be expected to come very soon and very early and not tie up large amounts of initial working capital. But if the product is one requiring a considerable educational campaign to get it established, then the firm must seriously consider whether or not it has the available funds to wait out the necessary length of time until the product begins to bring in an excess of revenue over costs paid out for its production and promotion.

Estimating the Value of an Investment Opportunity

Suppose your search for alternative investments had been thorough and reasonably complete and you had gone on to make the best and wisest forecast you could in each case of possible income and outlays involved. Are you now ready to make a profitable choice? Not until you have both a good yardstick for reducing all alternatives to the same common measure and some idea of what an acceptable opportunity should measure up to.

First, what kind of yardstick can we use to measure the relative value of different kinds of investments with different types of payouts and different lengths of economic life? There are two such major yardstick types that are widely known: the pay-back period, or the pay-back reciprocal, and the discounted rate of return on investment (also known as the discounted cash flow).

PAY-BACK PERIOD AND PAY-BACK RECIPROCAL

The most widely used standard for judging investment opportunities among businessmen is the pay-back period: How soon will the cost savings or other increased profits be paid back by the revenues from the investment? Or stated in equation form:

$$P = \frac{c}{r}$$

Where: P = number of years to recover cost
c = cost of investment
r = annual return on investment
(cost savings, additional profit on sales, or both)

This may be modified to define r as the annual return after taxes. The pay-back reciprocal is another variation of the same approach. This is simply a matter of inverting the equation and solving for r/c, the percentage of return of investment that will come back each year.

Pay-back is a rough-and-ready measure whose theoretical flaws have been thoroughly threshed over by many economists. But its virtues are worth looking at first. One of these is its simplicity and ease of comprehension. There is little ambiguity in the meaning of a pay-back. Another is that it is so obviously a simplified approximation that no one is likely to fool himself by thinking he has something really precise in the case of a decision that cannot be precise under any circumstances. Finally, it implicitly emphasizes the early return, the forecast returns closest in time and, therefore, open to the smallest degree of uncertainty.

Three theoretical objections are usually raised to the use of the pay-back yardstick:

1. It makes no overt distinction between investments with differing economic lives. Superficially, two investments of $30,000 are equal if they both return $15,000 a year even though the $15,000 is estimated to cease after some 30 months for the one but to continue for the next 30 years for the second.
2. The pay-back period ignores the need to discount returns for the time of their expected receipt.
3. The formula assumes return is uniform over time and this is not very probable.

But economic life does not have to be in the equation in order to be considered by the user and it is unlikely that many managers do not take estimated economic life into consideration when making their comparisons. Discounting of future returns is not taken into account directly but is implicit in the insistence that the total return be *more* than the payout. While a uniform cash flow is a simplification, it is probably the only reasonable assumption to make where cash flow is estimated over a considerable period of time. As will be shown below, the actual difference between the payout formulation and the theoretically-nice discounted cash flow concept may not be appreciable under certain realistic conditions.

There are other short cuts less widely used but with a blood relationship to payout. One of these is the first year performance standard, which puts the emphasis on return of incremental expenses, interest, and depreciation in the first year. Since it asks only for a minimum recovery of capital costs in the period in which the return is most certain, it obviously is not as adequate a standard as payoff.

PRESENT VALUE AND RATE OF RETURN

Useful as the payoff formula is for most simpler investment decisions, Dupont would probably have abandoned the development of nylon before it ever got out of the laboratory if payout had been the criterion for acceptance. Indeed, no really revolutionary innovation would stand the scrutiny of those who focus on the inevitable early year losses and low profits. Yet Dupont or any other enterprise would gladly bankroll any number of nylons it could find and afford. For, although the earliest profit trickle did not come till more than five years after the patent date, nylon is still a highly profitable and a developing product a quarter century later.

Of course not all innovations pay off like nylon, but the real payoff for any such revolutionary product will come only after years of physical and chemical research and development, more years of market cultivation, and large sums spent for sales promotion and industry service. Both the outlays and the returns are spread over time and nothing so sweet and easy as pay-back would be useful in evaluating complex projects such as these at each stage at which a decision has to be made. The principal complicating factor is the timing of outlays and revenue. The solution, therefore, is to use that universal measure of the lesser value of more distant revenue than current revenue: a discount rate.

There are two approaches using the discounting principle: (1) present value and (2) the discounted rate of return. Both will rate the same project profitable or otherwise and for the most part give the same result. Theoretically, however, they can yield different ranks of estimated value of any given group of alternate proposals. Those who like idle speculation may find some serious entertainment in arguing about which method is better. But every important parameter used in making this estimate of rate of return is subject to extreme variation and the very roughest of approximation. The rate of return itself is directly influenced by the estimate of the total returns to be expected and this can never be anything but rough, even for the near future. In addition, the estimate of economic life beyond the early years is little more than a guess and the salvage value in any distant future is nothing more. However precise the formulas and the tables based on the formulas, both present value and rate of return are just as much simplified approximations as the blunter-looking payout method. But they are the kind of approximations needed to really assess the value of more complex projects.

The best way to describe either of these methods is by means of their mathematical formulations.

Present Value

$$V = \frac{R_1}{1+i} + \frac{R_2}{(1+i)^2} + \ldots + \frac{R_n}{(1+i)^n} + \frac{S}{(1+i)^n}$$

V = present value
i = cost of capital (interest rate)
When: $R_1, R_2, \ldots, R_n$ = cash inflow after taxes for years $1, 2, \ldots, n$
S = salvage value of asset in year n.

Discounted Rate of Return

$$C = \frac{R_1}{1+r} + \frac{R_2}{(1+r)^2} + \ldots + \frac{R_n}{(1+r)^n} + \frac{S}{(1+r)^n}$$

When: r = discounted rate of return
C = cost of investment

Note that the precision of both of these approaches depends heavily on the accuracy of the forecasts of the R's (cash flows) for each and every year of the entire life of the asset, whether that asset be a physical process plant with a physical life of fifty years but subject to obsolescence by new development, or a new product the level of acceptance of which ten years from now is hardly an educated conjecture. Thus, although there have been various refinements developed on these formulas, their practical value is quite open to question. Furthermore, as theoretically nice as this method seems in contrast to the payoff period, it is still at least a distant cousin of the payoff formula itself. If, as often happens, we have to assume a relatively uniform rate of return, at least after an early period in the life of the asset, the rate of return r is equal to:

$$r = \frac{R}{C} - \frac{R}{C}\left(\frac{1}{1+r}\right)^n$$

Where: R = Annual rate of return
C = Investment cost

But the expression $\frac{1}{1-r}$ is less than 1 since r must always be a positive value. Thus there are two conditions in which the correction factor $\frac{R}{C}\left(\frac{1}{1+r}\right)^n$ approaches 0 and the value of x, therefore approaches the payoff reciprocal $\frac{R}{C}$: (1) when the estimated n, the economic life estimate, is large and (2) when the rate of return expected is large. As Spencer and Siegelman have pointed out in their development of this interesting relationship between payout and rate of return, very few businessmen will consider an investment that does not pay out approximately 20 percent before taxes, i.e., 10 percent after taxes. For projects with an economic life of even as little as five years, this makes the correction factor only ½ of 1 percent. For projects of ten years life, the correction becomes insignificant. In neither case is the actual payout estimate likely to be accurate enough to take account of such differences.

Probably the best approach where many alternatives are involved is to use some form of payout to sift down the alternatives to the ones that are most useful and then calculate the estimated rate of return. The latter is not really very difficult, since the actual calculation has already been done and put up in the form of present value tables and rate of return tables available in any financial text and in many other sources.

Other Methods of Evaluating Investments. There is only one other method widely known that seems to have some theoretical value and this is the well-known MAPI formula [1] proposed by the

[1] George Terbourgh, *Business Investment Policy* (Washington, D.C.: Machinery and Allied Products Institute, 1958).

economist George Terbourgh of Machine and Allied Product Institute. It is limited entirely to replacement decisions and takes into account some other factors.

Deciding on the Best Alternative

Some kind of list or ranking of projects will emerge, whatever the method of calculation. Should the manager accept the one that gives the best calculated rate of return? Not necessarily. These projects will undoubtably have different risk elements involved and also different lengths of economic life—an economic risk in and of itself regardless of other elements. Thus, one alternative with a discounted return of 12 percent for a two-year life may well be preferable to one with a rate of return figured over a twelve year life. The rate of return after the second year is much less certain and is more likely to be overestimated than underestimated. Thus the one with the shorter life would free the funds invested for other profitable investments much earlier than the one with the longer life, and the return expected could be counted on with greater certainty.

But time is not the only source of uncertainty. The reactions of competitors are not exactly predictable. The taste of customers, whether of the industrial or the final consumer type, can change radically in relatively short periods of time. And most important of all for any particular firm, some projects are likely to put it in a position to serve the market with something in which it has a major differential advantage while other projects are much less certain of resulting in any advantage over competitors.

Some subjective appraisal of the relative risks involved in making the investment must, therefore, be applied to the rate of return expected from each of the alternatives, introducing a still further degree of approximation into the investment decision. Having made allowance for the element of risk, the list will in all probability now have a different ranking.

At this point there are really just two useful bases of decision and they are far from being mutually exclusive. One approaches the question from the point of view of how much funds can be available for investment at a reasonable cost, and goes down the list as far as possible so long as it remains above this cost. The other simply sets a cut-off rate of return, e.g., 10 percent after taxes, above which a project must be considered. If the company is another American Telephone and Telegraph or Dupont, the latter method is quite likely to be the form used, the assumption being that if the project returns above this level, the company can always raise adequate funds in the market. For a smaller and less well-known firm this assumption may not be valid.

Learning from Your Mistakes and Successes

One nationally known firm used to have a cut-off rate of 24 percent before taxes but, curiously enough, none of the projects chosen ever came as high as 24 percent before tax yield. Few companies will be as consistent in underestimating or even over-estimating their prospects as this one, but many probably make a similar error of not carefully conducting a postmortem of previous decisions made and checking all of the assumptions that contributed to them. Forecasting of any sort is always a matter of carefully considered experience, and the most important part of any forecasting procedure is a careful reevaluation of the results of past decisions, not only in total, but in terms of each of the elements that contributed to the decision.

What Does the Money Cost?

Any rate of return assessment assumes some value for the cost of the money used. When the money is obtained from outside sources, this would seem to be rather easily determined; it is the cost actually paid, either in terms of the earnings ratio on stock sold or the interest paid to a lending institution. But investment almost invariably involves some use of internal funds and the question is raised as to what these internal funds are worth. There are doubtless some managers who consider the cost of such internal funds as insignificant since they already own them, but most are probably more economically sophisticated than this and realize that, even though they own the funds, there are other alternate uses that would yield some kind of profit. They can be loaned outside for government bonds, for example. Buying treasury notes or government bonds are a couple of the alternate opportunities a firm always has at its disposal and which may well be, in terms of the risk and return involved, the best temporary solution. However, any serious capital expenditure will normally yield a return far greater than this, even after risk is considered. Thus some other form of opportunity cost must be the basis for comparison. One usually suggested is to consider the rate of return the company might get on other investments on the same degree of risk. Philosophically this is a good solution. In practice, it is quite difficult to find really comparable investments with a really comparable degree of risk, except perhaps the common stocks available on the stock exchange. Another approach is simply to take alternative forms of investment available for the funds and apply an uncertainty or risk discount to the earnings obtained from these investments and from the projected alternatives. In any event, some value must be assigned and the decision is not likely to be a very precise one.

Some Important Aspects of the Capital Investment

TIMING THE INVESTMENT

In many decisions, the actual timing of the investment itself may have more to do with its ultimate success or failure than any other aspect of its handling. This is particularly true of investments involving new marketing operations, but also can be true of investments in which construction is a major item of cost. Unfortunately, the cost considerations and the marketing opportunity situations tend to clash in terms of optimum timing.

To take one example, consider the situation in the mail-order and retail field at the end of World War II. Every major company faced the need for some kind of major expansion if they were to take advantage of booming retail sales after the war. Incomes had risen drastically in many parts of the country, not only absolutely but relative to the situation before the war. All residential patterns had been uprooted and completely new ones were in the process of being established. The consuming public was famished for all sorts of durable and nondurable consumer goods. It was obviously a time in which retail businesses could be firmly established in new areas and new places. It was a time for market expansion and all four of the major general mail-order houses put under study some kinds of expansion plans, most particularly Montgomery Ward, Sears Roebuck, and Spiegel.

But it was also a time of skyrocketing construction costs. The cost of building new facilities and buying land was far out of line with what it had been a few years previously. Sears disregarded the construction costs on the philosophy that the time to build market was when markets were booming. They undertook major expansions not only in the United States, but in Central and South America. Montgomery Ward drew back, closing off units without replacing them, hoping to build later at a much lower cost in terms of both building and land. Spiegel seriously considered major expansion of its warehouse system and did expand by buying going retail establishments. But Spiegel recoiled at the cost of construction involved in new plants, hoping to get lower costs later.

The Sears strategy was right. The market opportunity was so important and the rise in construction costs so relatively permanent that Sears really got the cheapest expansion and the greatest expansion benefit. But there are other times when the costs far outweigh the possible benefits, and cost of construction or of money can change radically overnight.

There are also times, of course, when it is possible to move too soon, to get into a market before the market is ready for the particular kind of product. One major decision that must be made, then, is in what aspects of the decision timing is more important: the marketing aspect, where time must be seized by the forelock or the opportunity forever lost, or the cost aspect, where timing is so important that the success of the enterprise may be crippled by an unusually expensive investment base.

WORKING CAPITAL

The accountant defines working capital as the net current asset position, that is, the excess of current assets over current liabilities. In so defining working capital he is including two different types of capital, *start-up capital* needed to carry business until it gets onto its feet and what might be called *standpipe capital,* the liquid funds needed to bridge variations between cash flow and new liabilities. Unfortunately, most people starting businesses think of working capital primarily in terms of this standpipe concept, the amount of money needed simply to carry business once it gets going. The real problem in the use of working capital and in planning for it comes when businesses are new. In either situation, working capital may be defined more realistically as funds needed to bridge the gap between outlays incurred and subsequent revenues received from production. When a firm starts business, its expenses start immediately and often build up quite rapidly in the beginning. Revenue from sales inevitably comes later and often builds up very slowly and uncertainly for a considerable period. Sometimes, of course, revenues never become equal to outlays at a given time and the business fails because of too much optimism as to possible sales and profit margins. More often, the process takes much longer than the optimistic entrepreneur is apt to estimate. And although the business may have the potential of reaching the point where current revenues equal current outlays, he runs out of capital before this point is reached and the business flounders simply because it does not have sufficient capital to keep it afloat during the expansion period. Figure 7-1 (below), describes graphically the type of situation involved.

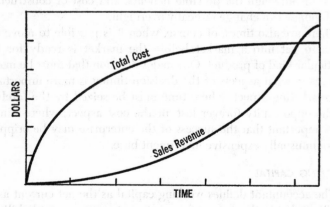

FIGURE 7-1. Typical Course of Expenditures and Sales in a Successful New Enterprise

Estimating the length of time necessary to get the business established and to get a volume sales return is, therefore, one of the most important elements in planning for working capital. This, in turn, requires a very careful estimate of the kind of product acceptance situation a company's plan is going to get it into—the length of time necessary to carry it over the period when only sample orders will be received from the small proportion of the market looking for something new.

Summary

1. The fact that the effects of any investment decision spread over time makes an estimate of these effects difficult. Choice of the best alternative necessitates careful search for all possible alternatives, wise forecasting of the expected income flows and outlays, choice of realistic methods of computing the cost of capital required and of estimating the present worth of each of the alternatives, choice of the proper standard of selection of alternatives, and post-audits of every decision to improve forecasting skill.

2. Insuring consideration of all possible alternatives requires a management attitude of constant search for new possibilities, a realization that the urgent day-to-day problems cannot be allowed to interfere with a longer look ahead, and constant safeguards against the inevitable bureaucratic attitude which develops in any large organization.

3. Forecasts must guard against the naive assumption that present trends and benefits are likely to persist indefinitely, particularly in cost reduction investment. The forecast of expected cash flows from major plant expansion, new products, and building new markets is especially difficult because assumptions must be made as to the future of consumer tastes and needs, and the actions of competitors.

4. There are two basic approaches to the estimate of the value of an investment: the pay-back period, and the discounted cash flow, or present worth, approach.

5. Pay-back asks, essentially, How soon will the expected income repay the outlay? It is simple, easy to understand, and it

emphasizes the much more certain early returns. Theoretically, it seems to disregard the differing economic lives of alternatives, after the pay-out period, and does not discount for the time of income receipt, but many of those who use it probably take these considerations into account in other ways. For simpler investments, it is probably adequate.

6. The rating of investments with longer term and delayed cash flows must be based on a method that takes into account the timing of those cash flows and the lesser value of a delayed dollar. The discounted cash flow is the proper form, or the very similar present worth calculation, both of which can be calculated from available tables.

7. The calculation will not automatically reveal the best choice for any given firm. The shorter term investment may be worth more than a seemingly equal longer term one because the income estimate is less likely to be overstated, and funds for future investment would be freed earlier. And account must be taken of the less measurable market aspects flowing from the decision such as which alternatives are in the direction in which the company can excel.

8. Forecasts of results are not accurate in any case and will improve only if past forecasts and their accuracy are audited.

9. Some form of opportunity cost must be used to evaluate the cost of the capital to be used, and there is no simple universal formula to do this.

10. Timing is an important aspect of any decision, and there is seldom any perfect time. Market considerations and cost considerations are seldom compatible, and the firm must decide which is of longer range importance.

11. Distinction must be made between working capital, needed for start-up costs, and standpipe working capital. Neglect of the importance of start-up capital is a common cause of failure of otherwise sound new ventures.

8

Tools Useful for Comparing Alternatives

EVEN WITH THE wisest use of the concepts so far discussed, determining which of the available opportunities will lead to the most desirable outcome is rarely easy, seldom a mere clerical calculation. The applicability and precision of available data *decreases* in direct ratio to the importance of an economic decision. But we can bring the meaning of what we can foresee about such outcomes into sharper focus with the use of certain mathematical tools, especially now that the computer has enabled us to avoid the tedium of calculation required by some of the more cumbersome of them. The actual operation of those techniques requiring much calculation or computer time is best left to those individuals who make such routines their everyday job, but the executive who uses the results will get no value from them, and may even be misled, if he does not have a thorough understanding of the nature, capabilities, and limits of the methods.

Fortunately, as with good tools of any kind, the principles involved are relatively simple. The four most important tools are:

1. sequential decision theory, useful in estimating the value of decision alternatives which train out over time
2. tools to determine the optimum timing of operations, primarily Gantt charts and network analysis
3. extremal methods—calculus and linear programming—to pinpoint the maximum and minimum combinations of factors and choices

4. Markov chain analysis to tell us where a dynamic situation is heading and what we can or should do about it.

Alternatives Occurring in a Time Sequence

Not infrequently, some of the alternatives open to us lead not to some definite outcome, but to the probability that other sets of alternatives will have to be considered, some of which may in turn lead to a definite outcome, but others to a need for further decisions before the final end can be seen.

It should be clear that in such a situation, some way of calculating the values of the final end result of all possible decision paths is needed if a rational choice is to be made. Let us consider a simplified example of such a situation. Suppose a man owns some land in the midst of a newly discovered oil field. A new value has now been added to this land; there is a possibility oil could be found under it, but not a certainty. He faces two choices immediately, if he desires to capitalize this new opportunity. He can sell a lease and get an immediate, certain profit. But the other alternative is to take some steps toward establishing the probability of oil, and even of drilling for himself. He can test for geological formation and, if the formation is favorable, sell the lease for a higher figure than before, for an immediate return, or take a chance and drill. If he drills, he may find oil, for a greater return than the lease would have brought, or he may hit a dry hole and get nothing. In either case, the outcome is final. Let us look at Figure 8-1 (page 183), a diagram of this sequence.

Which should the landowner do: sell the lease, test for formation, or drill? He has no means to arrive at a rational decision if this is the only information he has.

On the left hand side, he knows the payouts on the alternatives of selling the lease. But on the extreme right-hand path, the outcome of every decision has some degree of uncertainty. The test for formation may reveal a favorable formation, in which case the lease is worth more without going further, and the chance of getting oil if he himself drills is also better. But if the test is unfavorable, he has lost everything, including the added cost of the test. If he does drill himself, he adds another cost for drilling,

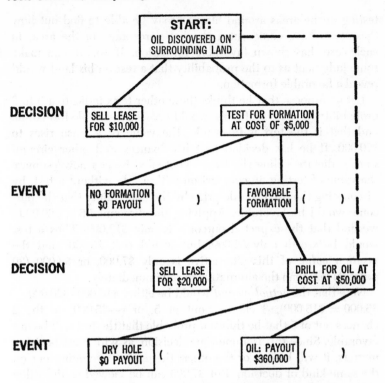

FIGURE 8-1. Possible Sequence of Decision and Event Alternatives in an Oil Lease Situation

and he may again lose everything, or get a big payoff. To know whether to test or to drill, he must somehow estimate the probability of finding a favorable formation, and the added probability of striking oil if he does. He thus needs some estimate of associated probabilities to fill in the blank brackets shown on the diagram; the probabilities that a favorable formation will be found, and the probability that oil will be struck if he does find formation.

He is not likely to find such information in any objective table of any kind. But he should have some data on which he can base a subjective estimate of both probabilities. If there has been any testing in the areas around him, he may be able to find out how these tests have come out and what percentage of the area, in each case, has shown favorable formation. If so, he can make some judgment as to the probability that a test on his land would reveal a favorable formation.

Let us suppose that he thinks these other tests indicate a 3 to 2 probability ($p = .6$) that a test would reveal a favorable formation, and that if the test is favorable, the value of a lease rises to $20,000. If he has decided that his finances and other circumstances dictate selling the lease eventually, he can now estimate the value of testing, in comparison with a sale without a test, by discounting the $20,000 sale price by the uncertainty that the outcome would be favorable. Applying the discount (.6 × $20,000), we find that the expected outcome is only $12,000. Thus a test would be worth only $2,000, but would cost $5,000, and the *position value* of this alternative is only $7,000, or $3,000 (30 percent) less than the alternative to sell immediately.

Note that the *actual payout* would be either $15,000 ($20,000 — $5,000 = $15,000), 3 chances out of 5, or (—$5,000) in the 2 chances out of 5 that he thinks it probable that the test will be unfavorable. Since this is a one-time decision, as with most business matters, it will be one or the other; there is no averaging out on the same kind of decision. But $7,000 can be viewed as the value of this alternative if considered to be one of a series of decisions of similar nature made on the basis of the same kind of information. If he were to make 100 such decisions—as a major oil operator might well do—and we simplify by assuming that the payout values would be the same in every case, and the costs, he would receive $1,000,000 net if he sold all such leases before test. But if he chose to test first in every case, he would incur a cost of $500,-000 for a gross return of $1,200,000 (60 × $20,000), or a net of only $700,000.

Both before and after such a test, however, the landowner can decide to do the drilling himself, rather than sell the lease to someone else who would drill. Such a decision would commit him to a further cost of $50,000. Is this option worth the cost, even if he can afford the commitment? To find out, he must have some further information, and make some further judgments as to the probability of success. Since the initial decision arose because of oil strikes on surrounding property, it should be easy to find out how many struck paying quantities of oil, and which did not. Assume that he finds that 1 out of 4 sunk into the favorable formation were paying wells, and that each such well had a capitalized value of $360,000.

If our landowner had made a test, and it was favorable, the value of a decision to drill rather than lease may then be estimated as:

(.25 × $360,000) — $50,000 = $90,000 — $50,000 = *$40,000*

| (The payout dis-counted for its uncertainty) | (Cost of drilling) | (Position value of the alternative to drill, after a favorable test) |

Once having made the test, and being fortunate enough to find favorable formation, then, the position value of the alternative to drill is thus worth twice the certain payout of $20,000 from the immediate sale of the lease. Working back to the initial situation, however, we must discount this position value by the risk of an unfavorable test, and the cost of the test itself:

(.6 × $40,000) — $5,000 = $24,000 — $5,000 = *$19,000*

With all due allowance for risks and costs, this alternative has a higher position value than the certain $10,000 to be received from the immediate sale of the lease before a test.

To get to this point, however, he spent $5,000 simply to get some information, information on whether the formation was favorable for the presence of oil. As we discovered already, this information was not worth $5,000 if the owner had decided to sell the lease anyway. Would it be worth $5,000 if the ultimate choice would be to drill? After all, the chance of finding formation seems to be better than even, anyway 3 to 5. In this case, the position value of the decision to drill immediately is determined by discounting the value of a well by the product of the two probabilities of finding formation, then of finding a well in a favorable formation, and subtracting the cost of drilling:

$$(.6 \times .25) \times \$360{,}000 - \$50{,}000 = .15 \times \$360{,}000 - \$50{,}000$$
$$= \$54{,}000 - \$50{,}000$$
$$= \$4{,}000$$

clearly less than the position value of the path test-then-drill-if-formation. The information gained from the test thus returns a value of $15,000 over its cost.

Note that in making these calculations, the sequence of calculations starts with the end point of a decision path, and works backward.

Figure 8-2 depicts graphically the three initial decision alternatives and the four decision paths which would result, together with costs and payouts. Comparing the four possible paths, we find that their position values are:

Path	Position Value (in Ms)	Probability of Success
Sell lease right away	$10	1.0
Test—then sell lease	7	.6
Drill immediately	4	.15
Test—then drill if favorable	19	.15

Clearly, the position value of test-then-drill is highest of the alternative decision paths. Is this the decision the landowner should make? Not necessarily. At this point, he must weigh some personal considerations not easily introduced into a mathematical formula (having used the latter to reveal the implications in his available objective information and subjective estimates translatable into reasonably objective form). The implications thus revealed are very helpful. They show that testing is not worth the cost if the end aim is to sell a lease anyway. On the other hand, the test is worth up to $20,000 in the information it gives, if the decision is to drill (the difference between the $24,000 gross position value of the test-then-drill alternative path, and the $4,000 position value of drill-immediately). They show that as between the other two alternatives, we are choosing between a certain value of $10,000 for immediate sale of the lease, and an alternative with an initial position value of $19,000, not between $10,000 and a well worth $360,000. And they bring into focus the reason for the difference

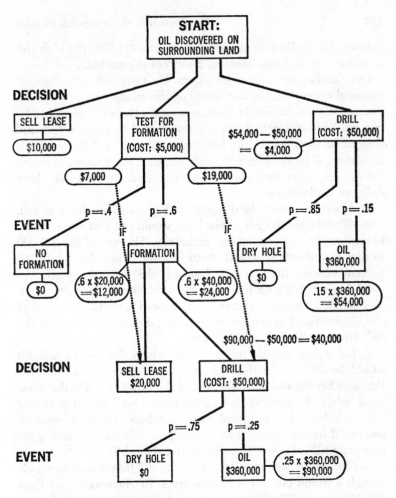

FIGURE 8-2. Completed Decision Tree, Showing all Possible Decision Paths with Estimated Decision Costs, Events with Estimated Probabilities, Actual Payouts, and Expected Values of the Payout in Reference to the Preceding Decision (Circled values are *expected values* for the preceding decision; *p* is the probability of the event)

between the well value of $360,000 and the $19,000: the high risk
of unsuccess, and the financial resources committed.

Our landowner must now assess his own *risk affordability,
financial resources, and the utility of the relative returns* to him.
The question of financial resources is easily disposed of; either he
has available $55,000 of risk capital needed to make a test and
drill, or he does not. In the latter case, he must sell the lease immediately. If he does have it available, then more subjective considerations come into play, best illustrated in terms of three
different landowners:

1. Alberts is a small landowner, with just this one lease to sell.
The $10,000 from the sale of the lease would put him in a position
to improve his own operations materially. The loss of the $55,000
in case of a dry hole would mean disaster. Since there is an 85
percent chance that he will lose all, the $10,000 certain has
much higher utility for him than the $19,000 position value of an
alternative with only a 15 percent chance of success, *even though
the $19,000 result is arrived at by taking objective account of the
risk.* His risk affordability is too low.

2. Baker is a wealthy neighbor, to whom the loss of $55,000
would be little more than an annoyance, even if the Internal
Revenue Service did not bear most of the brunt of it. On the other
hand, while the $360,000 from a successful well would probably
have relatively low marginal value for him, the excitement of
success, if he does bring it in, would probably have considerable
personal utility. He would probably test-then-drill.

3. Charleston can scrape together the $55,000, if necessary, al-
though it would take all of his resources. But he needs more than
$10,000 or even $55,000; he needs nearly $90,000 to stave off some
family disaster and pay for an operation needed if he is to live
more than another year. The $10,000 would have little value to
him. The $360,000 would salvage everything and give him a sub-
stantial stake in addition. Whatever the risk, he must go for broke.
He probably would drill immediately.

WHERE DO THE FIGURES COME FROM?

The mechanics of such a calculation are obviously not exotic.
Any bright grade school youngster could do the figuring, given

the figures. The essential problem is assigning something like the correct magnitude of value to the payouts and their probabilities. (The costs can usually be estimated with adequate accuracy.)

The quantities in our equations will nearly always be rough approximations. They may be based on empirical observations of only somewhat similar or analogous situations, adjusted on the basis of the kind of personal feeling or hunch that grows out of the accumulation of minor, usually subconscious, experiences which give us a feel of the market. They may be inferences drawn from various kinds of available objective data, e.g., in our example, the experience of other testing and drilling operations in the neighborhood; or census tabulations, trade statistics, or personal observations made by those familiar with the kind of situation with which a decision is concerned.

They should never be arbitrary guesses pulled out of the air, and all adjustments made on any objective base data used should have a supportable logic. Wherever we get our figures, we must check their credibility and their relevance to the kind of decision with which we are confronted.

Seldom will our figures have any high degree of precision; at most, they will usually express some sort of rough maximum or minimum. Our landowner thought that the probability of finding a favorable formation was .6 on the basis of the best information he could get. He probably meant "at least .6," and did not imply the figure could not have been as low as .54, for example, or that it could not have been as high as .8. If such an initial statement leaves too high a range of uncertainty to permit of decision choice, the best decision is probably to seek additional information before acting. Otherwise, we are taking a gamble, not a calculated risk. We are permitting the outcome to be decided by the net effect of an infinity of minor factors that mathematicians sum up under the term *random*. In the long run, the true gambler always loses out to the certainty of the house percentage.

WHAT DO THE RESULTS TELL US?

Putting down some probability figures and performing the arithmetic confers no particular magic. The process can lead to false confidence if the figures alone are thought to be able to carry the weight of the decision. The real value of the process is often in trying to arrive at as accurate a representation as possible of the quantitative significance of all the data we have which we think pertinent to the decision, at a specific measure of the kinds of risks we think are involved, and at the size of the payouts we have a right to expect. When you must put down a specific figure *and justify it*, you are more likely to hone your thinking to a finer edge than when you are allowed to get away with some comfortably vague generalizations.

Calculations carried out on figures furnished in this spirit can then reveal to us the relative monetary value of different decision sequences and thus help us choose a decision path that will optimize the kinds of results consonant with the firm's objectives, capabilities, and situation.

Optimizing Timing of Task Components

Time resources are often the critical element in ultimate success in highly complex universe of our industrial production and distribution systems. Timing was important even in an agricultural civilization to the profitable conduct of planting, cultivation, and harvest. But the farmer's timing problems are absurdly simple compared with those facing enterprise in a nationwide marketing system. The traditional agriculturist could safely follow rules of thumb developed out of generations of experience in his particular district. The enterprise facing daily changes in processes and products has no established rules of thumb that can safely be followed. To keep our complex industrial machinery rolling smoothly, industry has been compelled to develop techniques for analysis of the timing requirements and optimization of the timing of components of a complicated task.

The basic principle of time optimization is the same, whether we use Gantt's original Chart which he developed to aid the World War I Shipping Board create a merchant fleet overnight, or today's lineal descendants of this genius' insight: the *network analysis* methods of CPM and PERT. All aim at (1) making sure that the job can proceed or is proceeding on a schedule that will meet a desired deadline and (2) finding the most economical and quickest path to that deadline. They all start by dividing the entire job into its most elementary component tasks, estimating the time necessary to carry out each of these tasks, their sequential interrelationships, and necessary starting and ending times in relation to these sequences.

The original *Gantt Chart* was, as the name implies, essentially a graphic device giving a visual representation of time requirements and progress of each component in relation to those requirements. In one form or another, the Gantt Chart has become a standard tool of production control.

Network analysis has been developed to aid in the planning and execution of the more complex development, construction, and production processes for which such a simple graphic device would be inadequate. The two principal forms have been designated the Critical Path Method (CPM) and Program Review and Evaluation Technique (PERT). The main difference between CPM and PERT is the use of probability values for both time and cost in PERT. The latter was developed originally for application to research and development projects in which such quantities cannot be estimated very accurately. Both use the same basic approach, which has been well summarized in the following article by Levy, Thompson, and Wiest.

THE ABCS OF THE CRITICAL PATH METHOD [1]

FERDINAND K. LEVY
GERALD L. THOMPSON
JEROME D. WIEST

Recently added to the growing assortment of quantitative tools for business decision making is the Critical Path Method—a powerful but basically simple technique for analyzing, planning, and scheduling

AUTHORS' NOTE: The preparation of this article was supported by the Office of Naval Research and the Bureau of Ships through grants to the Graduate School of Industrial Administration, Carnegie Institute of Technology. A different version of this material appears as Chapter 20 in *Industrial Scheduling*, edited by J. F. Muth and G. L. Thompson (Englewood Cliffs, New Jersey, Prentice-Hall, Inc., 1963). The job list and project graph for the house-building example were developed by Peter R. Winters.

[1] [Reprinted from the *Harvard Business Review*, Vol. 41, No. 5 (September-October, 1963), pp. 98-108].

large, complex projects. In essence, the tool provides a means of determining (1) which jobs or activities, of the many that comprise a project, are "critical" in their effect on total project time, and (2) how best to schedule all jobs in the project in order to meet a target date at minimum cost. Widely diverse kinds of projects lend themselves to analysis by CPM, as is suggested in the following list of applications:

- The construction of a building (or a highway).
- Planning and launching a new product.
- A turnaround in an oil refinery (or other maintenance projects).
- Installing and debugging a computer system.
- Research and engineering design projects.
- Scheduling ship construction and repairs.
- The manufacture and assembly of a large generator (or other job-lot operations).
- Missile countdown procedures.

Each of these projects has several characteristics that are essential for analysis by CPM:

(1) The project consists of a well-defined collection of jobs (or activities) which, when completed, mark the end of the project.
(2) The jobs may be started and stopped independently of each other, within a given sequence. (This requirement eliminates continuous-flow process activities, such as oil refining, where "jobs" or operations necessarily follow one after another with essentially no slack.)
(3) The jobs are ordered—that is, they must be performed in technological sequence. (For example, the foundation of a house must be constructed before the walls are erected.)

WHAT IS THE METHOD?

The concept of CPM is quite simple and may best be illustrated in terms of a project graph. The graph is not an essential part of CPM; computer programs have been written which permit necessary calculations to be made without reference to a graph. Nevertheless, the project graph is valuable as a means of depicting, visually and clearly, the complex of jobs in a project and their interrelations:

First of all, each job necessary for the completion of a project is listed with a unique identifying symbol (such as a letter or number), the time required to complete the job, and its immediate prerequisite jobs. For convenience in graphing, and as a check on certain kinds of data errors, the jobs may be arranged in "technological order," which means that no job appears on the list until all of its predecessors have been listed. Technological ordering is impossible if a cycle error exists in the job data (e.g., job a precedes b, b precedes c, and c precedes a).

Then each job is drawn on the graph as a circle, with its identifying symbol and time appearing within the circle. Sequence relationships are indicated by arrows connecting each circle (job) with its immediate successors, with the arrows pointing to the latter. For convenience, all circles with no predecessors are connected to a circle marked "Start"; likewise, all circles with no successors are connected to a circle marked "Finish." (The "Start" and "Finish" circles may be considered pseudo jobs of zero time length.)

Typically, the graph then depicts a number of different "arrow paths" from Start to Finish. The time required to traverse each path is the sum of the times associated with all jobs on the path. The critical path (or paths) is the longest path (in time) from Start to Finish; it indicates the minimum time necessary to complete the entire project.

This method of depicting a project graph differs in some respects from that used by James E. Kelley, Jr., and Morgan R. Walker, who, perhaps more than anyone else, were responsible for the initial development of CPM. (For an interesting account of its early history see their paper, "Critical-Path Planning and Scheduling." [*] In the widely used Kelley-Walker form, a project graph is just the opposite of that described above: jobs are shown as arrows, and the arrows are connected by means of circles (or dots) that indicate sequence relationships. Thus all immediate predecessors of a given job connect to a circle at the tail of the job arrow, and all immediate successor jobs emanate from the circle at the head of the job arrow. In essence, then, a circle marks an event—the completion of all jobs leading into the circle. Since these jobs are the immediate prerequisites for all jobs leading out of the circle, they must all be completed before *any* of the succeeding jobs can begin.

In order to accurately portray all predecessor relationships, "dummy jobs" must often be added to the project graph in the Kelley-Walker

[*] *Proceedings of the Eastern Joint Computer Conference*, Boston, December 1-3, 1959; see also James E. Kelley, Jr., "Critical-Path Planning and Scheduling: Mathematical Basis," *Operations Research*, May-June 1961, pp. 296-320.

form. The method described in this article avoids the necessity and complexity of dummy jobs, is easier to program for a computer, and also seems more straightforward in explanation and application.

In essence, the critical path is the bottleneck route. Only by finding ways to shorten jobs along the critical path can the over-all project time be reduced; the time required to perform noncritical jobs is irrelevant from the viewpoint of total project time. The frequent (and costly) practice of "crashing" *all* jobs in a project in order to reduce total project time is thus unnecessary. Typically, only about 10% of the jobs in large projects are critical. (This figure will naturally vary from project to project.) Of course, if some way is found to shorten one or more of the critical jobs, then not only will the whole project time be shortened but the critical path itself may shift and some previously noncritical jobs may become critical.

EXAMPLE: BUILDING A HOUSE

A simple and familiar example should help to clarify the notion of critical path scheduling and the process of constructing a graph. The project of building a house is readily analyzed by the CPM technique and is typical of a large class of similar applications. While a contractor might want a more detailed analysis, we will be satisfied here with the list of major jobs (together with the estimated time and the immediate predecessors for each job) shown in Exhibit 8-1.

In that exhibit, the column "immediate predecessors" determines the sequence relationships of the jobs and enables us to draw the project graph, Exhibit 8-2. Here, in each circle the letter before the comma identifies the job and the number after the comma indicates the job time.

Following the rule that a "legal" path must always move in the direction of the arrows, we could enumerate 22 unique paths from Start to Finish, with associate times ranging from a minimum of 14 days (path *a-b-c-r-v-w-x*) to a maximum of 34 days (path *a-b-c-d-j-k-l-n-t-s-x*). The latter is the critical path; it determines the over-all project time and tells us which jobs are critical in their effect on this time. If the contractor wishes to complete the house in less than 34 days, it would be useless to shorten jobs not on the critical path. It may seem to him, for example, that the brickwork (*e*) delays progress, since work on a whole series of jobs (*p-q-v-w*) must wait until it is completed. But

EXHIBIT 8-1. Sequence and Time Requirement of Jobs

JOB NO.	DESCRIPTION	IMMEDIATE PREDECESSORS	NORMAL TIMES (DAYS)
a	START		0
b	EXCAVATE AND POUR FOOTERS	a	4
c	POUR CONCRETE FOUNDATION	b	2
d	ERECT WOODEN FRAME INCLUDING ROUGH ROOF	c	4
e	LAY BRICKWORK	d	6
f	INSTALL BASEMENT DRAINS AND PLUMBING	c	1
g	POUR BASEMENT FLOOR	f	2
h	INSTALL ROUGH PLUMBING	f	3
i	INSTALL ROUGH WIRING	d	2
j	INSTALL HEATING AND VENTILATING	d,g	4
k	FASTEN PLASTER BOARD AND PLASTER (INCLUDING DRYING)	i,j,h	10
l	LAY FINISH FLOORING	k	3
m	INSTALL KITCHEN FIXTURES	l	1
n	INSTALL FINISH PLUMBING	l	2
o	FINISH CARPENTRY	l	3
p	FINISH ROOFING AND FLASHING	e	2
q	FASTEN GUTTERS AND DOWNSPOUTS	p	1
r	LAY STORM DRAINS FOR RAIN WATER	c	1
s	SAND AND VARNISH FLOORING	o,t	2
t	PAINT	m,n	3
u	FINISH ELECTRICAL WORK	t	1
v	FINISH GRADING	q,r	2
w	POUR WALKS AND COMPLETE LANDSCAPING	v	5
x	FINISH	s,u,w	0

EXHIBIT 8-2. Project Graph

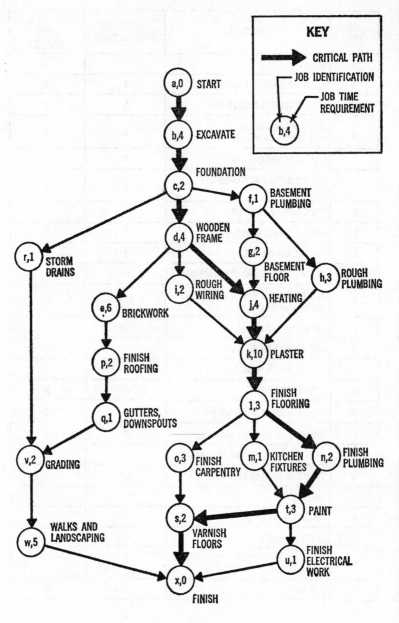

it would be fruitless to rush the completion of the brickwork, since it is not on the critical path and so is irrelevant in determining total project time.

Shortening the CP

If the contractor were to use CPM techniques, he would examine the critical path for possible improvements. Perhaps he could assign more carpenters to job *d*, reducing it from four to two days. Then the critical path would change slightly, passing through jobs *f* and *g* instead of *d*. Notice that total project time would be reduced only one day, even though two days had been shaved off job *d*. Thus the contractor must watch for possible shifting of the critical path as he affects changes in critical jobs.

Shortening the critical path requires a consideration of both engineering problems and economic questions. Is it physically possible to shorten the time required by critical jobs (by assigning more men to the job, working overtime, using different equipment, and so on)? If so, would the costs of speedup be less than the savings resulting from the reduction in over-all project time? CPM is a useful tool because it quickly focuses attention on those jobs that are critical to the project time, it provides an easy way to determine the effects of shortening various jobs in the project, and it enables the user to evaluate the costs of a "crash" program.

Two important applications of these features come to mind:

¶ Du Pont, a pioneer in the application of CPM to construction and maintenance projects, was concerned with the amount of downtime for maintenance at its Louisville works, which produces an intermediate product in the neoprene process. Analyzing the maintenance schedule by CPM, Du Pont engineers were able to cut downtime for maintenance from 125 to 93 hours. CPM pointed to further refinements that were expected to reduce total time to 78 hours. As a result, performance of the plant improved by about one million pounds in 1959, and the intermediate was no longer a bottleneck in the neoprene process.

¶ PERT (i.e., Program Evaluation Review Technique), a technique closely related to the critical path method, is widely credited with helping to shorten by two years the time originally estimated for completion of the engineering and development program for the Navy's Polaris missile. By pinpointing the longest paths through the vast maze of jobs necessary for completion of the missile design, PERT enabled the program managers to concentrate their efforts on those activities that vitally affected total project time.*

Even with our small house-building project, however, the process of enumerating and measuring the length of every path through the maze of jobs is tedious. A simple method of finding the critical path and, at the same time, developing useful information about each job is described next.

CRITICAL PATH ALGORITHM

If the start time or date for the project is given (we denote it by S), then there exists for each job an earliest starting time (ES), which is the earliest possible time that a job can begin, if all its predecessors are also started at their ES. And if the time to complete the job is t, we can define, analogously, its earliest finish time (EF) to be ES + t.

There is a simple way of computing ES and EF times using the project graph. It proceeds as follows:

(1) Mark the value of S to the left and to the right of Start.
(2) Consider any new unmarked job *all of whose predecessors have been marked,* and mark to the left of the new job the *largest* number marked to the right of any of its *immediate* predecessors. This number is its early start time.
(3) Add to this number the job time and mark the result (EF time) to the right of the job.
(4) Continue until Finish has been reached, then stop.

Thus, at the conclusion of this calculation the ES time for each job will appear to the left of the circle which identifies it, and the EF time will appear to the right of the circle. The number which appears to the right of the last job, Finish, is the early finish time (F) for the entire project.

To illustrate these calculations let us consider the following simple production process:

An assembly is to be made from two parts, A and B. Both parts must be turned on the lathe, and B must be polished while A need not be. The list of jobs to be performed, together with the predecessors of

---

* See Robert W. Miller, "How to Plan and Control With PERT," HBR March-April 1962, p. 93.

each job and the time in minutes to perform each job, is given in Exhibit 8-3.

EXHIBIT 8-3. Data for Production Process

JOB NO.	DESCRIPTION	IMMEDIATE PREDECESSORS	NORMAL TIMES (MINUTES)
a	START		0
b	GET MATERIALS FOR A	a	10
c	GET MATERIALS FOR B	a	20
d	TURN A ON LATHE	b,c	30
e	TURN B ON LATHE	b,c	20
f	POLISH B	e	40
g	ASSEMBLE A AND B	d,f	20
h	FINISH	g	0

The project graph is shown in Exhibit 8-4. As previously, the letter identifying each job appears before the comma and its job time after the comma. Also shown on the graph are the ES and EF times for each job, assuming that the start time, S, is *zero*. The ES time appears to the left of the circle representing a job, and the EF time appears to the right of the circle. Note that F = 100. The reader may wish to duplicate the diagram without these times and carry out the calculations for himself as a check on his understanding of the computation process described above.

Latest Start & Finish Times

Suppose now that we have a target time (T) for completing the project. T may have been originally expressed as a calendar date, e.g., October 1 or February 15. When is the latest time that the project can be started and finished?

In order to be feasible it is clear that T must be greater (later) than or equal to F, the early finish time for the project. Assuming this is so, we can define the concept of late finish (LF), or the latest time that a job can be finished, without delaying the total project beyond its target

EXHIBIT 8-4. Calculation of Early Start and Early Finish Times for Each Job

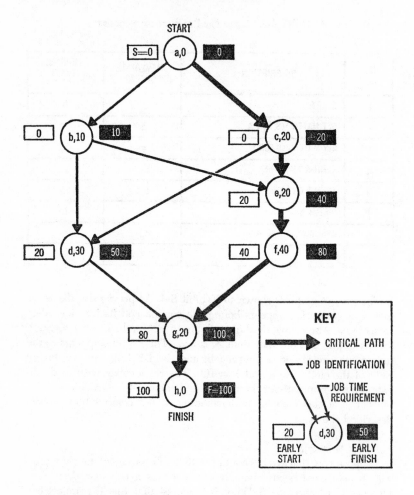

time (T). Similarly, late start (LS) is defined to be LF − t, where t is the job time.

These numbers are determined for each job in a manner similar to the previous calculations except that we work from the end of the project to its beginning. We proceed as follows:

(1) Mark the value of T to the right and left of Finish.
(2) Consider any new unmarked job *all of whose successors have been marked,* and mark to the right of the new job the *smallest* LS time marked to the left of any of its immediate successors.

The logic of this is hard to explain in a few words, although apparent enough by inspection. It helps to remember that the smallest LS time of the successors of a given job, if translated into calendar times, would be the latest finish time of that job.
(3) Subtract from this number the job time and mark the result to the left of the job.
(4) Continue until Start has been reached, then stop.

At the conclusion of this calculation the LF time for a job will appear to the right of the circle which identifies it, and the LS time for the job will appear to the left of the circle. The number appearing to the right of Start is the latest time that the entire project can be started and still finish at the target time T.

In Exhibit 8-5 we carry out these calculations for the example of Exhibit 8-3. Here T = F = 100, and we separate early start and finish and late start and finish times by semicolons so that ES; LS appears to the left of the job and EF; LF to the right. Again the reader may wish to check these calculations for himself.

CONCEPT OF SLACK

Examination of Exhibit 8-5 reveals that some jobs have their early start equal to late start, while others do not. The difference between a job's early start and its late start (or between early finish and late finish) is called total slack (TS). Total slack represents the maximum amount of time a job may be delayed beyond its early start without necessarily delaying the project completion time.

We earlier defined critical jobs as those on the longest path through the project. That is, critical jobs *directly* affect the total project time. We can now relate the critical path to the concept of slack.

Finding the Critical Path
If the target date (T) equals the early finish date for the whole project (F), then all critical jobs will have *zero* total slack. There will be at least one path going from Start to Finish that includes critical jobs only, i.e., the *critical path.*

**EXHIBIT 8-5. Calculation of Late Start and Late Finish
Times for Each Job**

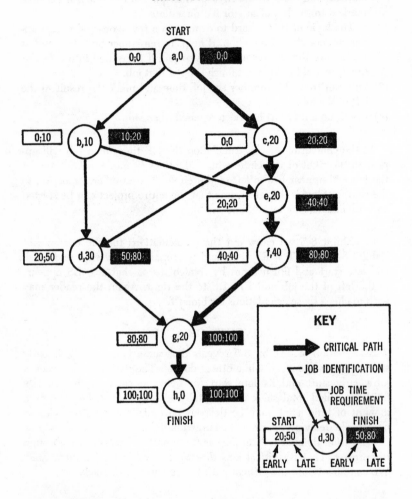

If T is greater (later) than F, then the critical jobs will have total slack equal to T minus F. This is a minimum value; since the critical path includes only critical jobs, it includes those with the smallest TS. All noncritical jobs will have *greater* total slack.

In Exhibit 8-5, the critical path is shown by darkening the arrows connecting critical jobs. In this case there is just one critical path, and all critical jobs lie on it; however, in other cases there may be more than one critical path. Note that T = F; thus the critical jobs have zero total slack. Job b has TS = 10, and job d has TS = 30; either or both of these jobs could be delayed by these amounts of time without delaying the project.

Another kind of slack is worth mentioning. Free slack (FS) is the amount a job can be delayed without delaying the early start of any other job. A job with positive total slack may or may not also have free slack, but the latter never exceeds the former. For purposes of computation, the free slack of a job is defined as the difference between the job's EF time and the *earliest* of the ES times of all its immediate successors. Thus, in Exhibit 8-5, job b has FS of 10, and job d has FS of 30. All other jobs have zero free slack.

Significance of Slack

When a job has zero total slack, its scheduled start time is automatically fixed (that is, ES = LS); and to delay the calculated start time is to delay the whole project. Jobs with positive total slack, however, allow the scheduler some discretion in setting their start times. This flexibility can usefully be applied to smoothing work schedules. Peak loads that develop in a particular shop (or on a machine, or within an engineering design group, to cite other examples) may be relieved by shifting jobs on the peak days to their late starts. Slack allows this kind of juggling without affecting project time.*

Free slack can be used effectively at the operating level. For example, if a job has free slack, the foreman may be given some flexibility in deciding when to start the job. Even if he delays the start by an amount equal to (or less than) the free slack, the delay will not affect the start times or slack of succeeding jobs (which is not true of jobs that have no free slack). For an illustration of these notions, we return to our house-building example.

Back to the Contractor

In Exhibit 8-6, we reproduce the diagram of house-building jobs, marking the ES and LS to the left, and the EF and LF to the right of each job (for example, "0;3" and "4;7" on either side of the b,4 circle).

---

* For a method for smoothing operations in a job shop, based on CPM and the use of slack, see F. K. Levy, G. L. Thompson, and J. D. Wiest, "Multi-ship, Multi-Shop Production Smoothing Algorithm," *Naval Logistics Research Quarterly*, March 9, 1962.

We assume that construction begins on day zero and must be completed by day 37. Total slack for each job is not marked, since it is evident as the difference between the pairs of numbers ES and LS or EF and LF. However, jobs that have positive free slack are so marked. There is one critical path, which is shown darkened in the diagram. All critical jobs on this path have total slack of three days.

Several observations can be drawn immediately from the diagram:

(1) The contractor could postpone starting the house three days and still complete it on schedule, barring unforeseen difficulties (see the difference between early and late times at the Finish.) This would reduce the total slack of all jobs by three days, and hence reduce TS for critical jobs to zero.

(2) Several jobs have free slack. Thus the contractor could delay the completion of i (rough wiring) by two days, g (the basement floor) by one day, h (rough plumbing) by four days, r (the storm drains) by 12 days, and so on—without affecting succeeding jobs.

(3) The series of jobs e (brickwork), p (roofing), q (gutters), v (grading), and w (landscaping) have a comfortable amount of total slack (nine days). The contractor can use these and other slack jobs as "fill in" jobs for workers who become available when their skills are not needed for currently critical jobs. This is a simple application of workload smoothing: juggling the jobs with slack in order to reduce peak demands for certain skilled workers or machines.

If the contractor were to effect changes in one or more of the critical jobs, by contrast, the calculations would have to be performed again. This he can easily do; but in large projects with complex sequence relationships, hand calculations are considerably more difficult and liable to error. Computer programs have been developed, however, for calculating ES, LS, EF, LF, TS, and FS for each job in a project, given the set of immediate prerequisites and the job times for each job.*

HANDLING DATA ERRORS

Information concerning job times and predecessor relationships is gathered, typically, by shop foremen, scheduling clerks, or others

---

* An algorithm on which one such computer program is based is discussed by F. K. Levy, G. L. Thompson, and J. D. Wiest, in chapter 22, "Mathematical Basis of the Critical Path Method," *Industrial Scheduling* (see Authors' Note, p. 192).

EXHIBIT 8-6. Project Graph with Start and Finish Times

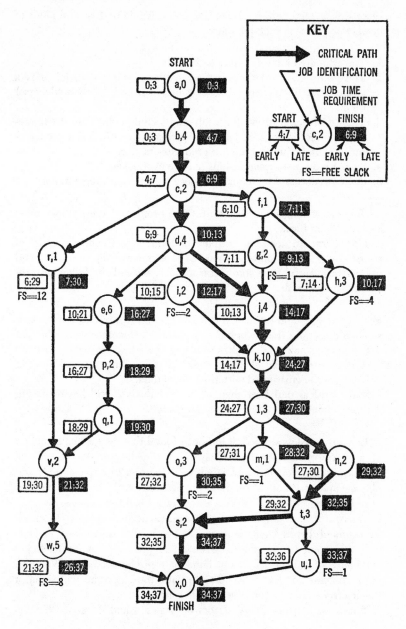

closely associated with a project. It is conceivable that several kinds of errors may occur in such job data:

1. The estimated job times may be in error.
2. The predecessor relationship may contain cycles: e.g., job a is a predecessor for b, b is a predecessor for c, and c is a predecessor for a.
3. The list of prerequisites for a job may include more than the immediate prerequisites; e.g., job a is a predecessor of b, b is a predecessor of c, and a and b both are predecessors of c.
4. Some predecessor relationships may be overlooked.
5. Some predecessor relationships may be listed that are spurious.

How can management deal with these problems? We shall examine each briefly in turn.

Job Times. An accurate estimate of total project time depends, of course, on accurate job-time data. CPM eliminates the necessity (and expense) of careful time studies for *all* jobs. Instead the following procedure can be used:

- Given rough time estimates, construct a CPM graph of the project.
- Then those jobs that are on the critical path (together with jobs that have very small total slack, indicating that they are nearly critical) can be more closely checked, their times re-estimated, and another CPM graph constructed with the refined data.
- If the critical path has changed to include jobs still having rough time estimates, then the process is repeated.

In many projects studied, it has been found that only a small fraction of jobs are critical; so it is likely that refined time studies will be needed for relatively few jobs in a project in order to arrive at a reasonably accurate estimate of the total project time. CPM thus can be used to reduce the problem of Type 1 errors at a small total cost.

Prerequisites. A computer algorithm has been developed to check for errors of Types 2 and 3 above. The algorithm (mentioned in footnote 4) systematically examines the set of prerequisites for each job and cancels from the set all but immediate predecessor jobs. When an error of Type 2 is present in the job data, the algorithm will signal a "cycle error" and print out the cycle in question.

Wrong or Missing Facts. Errors of Types 4 and 5 cannot be discovered by computer routines. Instead, manual checking (perhaps by a committee) is necessary to see that prerequisites are accurately reported.

COST CALCULATIONS

The cost of carrying out a project can be readily calculated from the job data if the cost of doing each job is included in the data. If jobs are done by crews, and the speed with which the job is done depends on the crew size, then it is possible to shorten or lengthen the project time by adding or removing men from crews. Other means for compressing job times might also be found; but any speedup is likely to carry a price tag. Suppose that we assign to each job a "normal time" and a "crash time" and also calculate the associated costs necessary to carry the job in each time. If we want to shorten the project, we can assign some of the critical jobs to their crash time, and compute the corresponding direct cost. In this way it is possible to calculate the cost of completing the project in various total times, with the direct costs increasing as the over-all time decreases.

Added to direct costs are certain overhead expenses which are usually allocated on the basis of total project time. Fixed costs per project thus decrease as project time is shortened. In ordinary circumstances a combination of fixed and direct costs as a function of total project time would probably fall into the pattern shown in Exhibit 8-7. The minimum total cost (point A) would likely fall to the left of the minimum point on the direct cost curve (point B) indicating that the optimum project time is somewhat shorter than an analysis of direct costs only would indicate.

Other economic factors, of course, can be included in the analysis. For example, pricing might be brought in:

A large chemical company starts to build a plant for producing a new chemical. After the construction schedule and completion date are established, an important potential customer indicates a willingness to pay a premium price for the new chemical if it can be made available earlier than scheduled. The chemical producer applies techniques of CPM to its construction schedule and calculates the additional costs associated with "crash" completion of jobs on the critical path. With a plot of costs correlated with total project time, the producer is able to select a new completion date such that the increased costs are met by the additional revenue offered by the customer.

EXHIBIT 8-7. Typical Cost Pattern

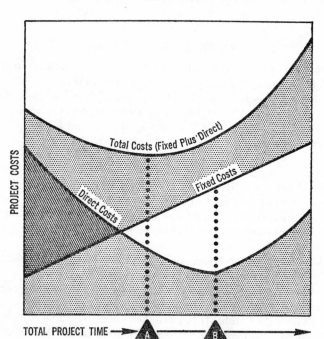

NEW DEVELOPMENTS

Because of their great potential for applications, both CPM and PERT have received intensive development in the past few years. This effort is sparked, in part, because of the Air Force (and other governmental agency) requirements that contractors use these methods in planning and monitoring their work. Here are some illustrations of progress made:

¶ One of the present authors (Wiest) has developed extensions of the work-load smoothing algorithm. These extensions are the so-called SPAR (for Scheduling Program for Allocating Resources) programs for scheduling projects having limited resources.

¶ A contemporaneous development by C-E-I-R, Inc., has produced

RAMPS (for Resource Allocation and Multi-Project Scheduling), which is similar but not identical.

¶ The most recent version of PERT, called PERT/COST, was developed by the armed services and various businesses for use on weapon-systems development projects contracted by the government. Essentially, PERT/COST adds the consideration of resource costs to the schedule produced by the PERT procedure. Indications of how smoothing can be accomplished are also made. Other recent versions are called PERT II, PERT III, PEP, PEPCO, and Super PERT.

CONCLUSION

For the manager of large projects, CPM is a powerful and flexible tool, indeed, for decision making:

- It is useful at various stages of project management, from initial planning or analyzing of alternative programs, to scheduling and controlling the jobs (activities) that comprise a project.
- It can be applied to a great variety of project types—from our house-building example to the vastly more complicated design project for the Polaris—and at various levels of planning—from scheduling jobs in a single shop, or shops in a plant, to scheduling plants within a corporation.
- In a simple and direct way it displays the interrelations in the complex of jobs that comprise a large project.
- It is easily explainable to the layman by means of the project graph. Data calculations for large projects, while tedious, are not difficult, and can readily be handled by a computer.
- It pinpoints attention to the small subset of jobs that are critical to project completion time, thus contributing to more accurate planning and more precise control.
- It enables the manager to quickly study the effects of "crash" programs and to anticipate potential bottlenecks that might result from shortening certain critical jobs.
- It leads to reasonable estimates of total project costs for various completion dates, which enable the manager to select an optimum schedule.

Because of the above characteristics of CPM—and especially its intuitive logic and graphic appeal—it is a decision-making tool which can find wide appreciation at all levels of management.* The project graph helps the foreman to understand the sequencing of jobs and the necessity of pushing those that are critical. For the manager concerned with day-to-day operations in all departments, CPM enables him to measure progress (or lack of it) against plans and to take appropriate action quickly when needed. And the underlying simplicity of CPM and its ability to focus attention on crucial problem areas of large projects make it an ideal tool for the top manager. On his shoulders falls the ultimate responsibility for over-all planning and coordination of such projects in the light of company-wide objectives.

Pinpointing the Optimum Point or Optimum Input Mix

Seldom does the executive face the simple choice between the clearly profitable and the obviously unprofitable. More usually, he must judge which of a number of possibilities is the more profitable or the least costly, or some other extreme of desirability. Mathematics offers two general types of tools for determination of such *extremal points,* if suitable data is available: (1) *differential calculus* when the relationships are known and are nonlinear, and (2) *linear programming* when the relationships are known and can be expressed in linear form. There is also a form of mathematical programming for nonlinear relationships, but no fruitful application of this approach has come to light. In every case, of course, there must be a known relationship, stated in quantitative terms of parametric quality.

Calculus has played such a valuable role in the study of the physical sciences that it is only human to hope that it would prove of comparable value in business decision and, at first blush, it would seem applicable. Indeed, most of the discussion of economic price theory, and of marginal analysis in general, has made use of this approach, although usually in terms of the graphic equivalent, rather than the normal symbolic form. The maxima and minima determined by setting the derivative equal to zero are seen as the horizontal turning points on a graphed curve. Un-

---

* See A. Charnes and W. W. Cooper, "A Network Interpretation and a Directed Sub-Dual Algorithm for Critical Path Scheduling," *Journal of Industrial Engineering*, July-August 1962, pp. 213-219.

fortunately, in actual life, we seldom or never have available the kind of data needed to make use of such precise supply and demand curves, and what information we do get indicates that the relationship between price and consumer reaction seldom follows the smoothly changing curves found in our textbooks and necessary to the use of calculus.

Furthermore, within the range of values in which business decision is free to operate, many factor relationships prove to be close to linear in form, not curvilinear as required for the use of calculus. Fortunately, data available from many repetitive operating level situations are suitable for linear programming calculation.

Linear programming permits the discovery of any possible extremal points if known relationships and requirements are either linear in form or can be transformed into linear form by any of the simpler mathematical tricks. Most operating relationships and requirements are of this form. Within plant or shift capacity limits, variable production costs tend to be linear, and so do many price-quantity relationships within the narrow range open to decision. Many decision requirements are in the form of linear *restraints,* the stipulation that they be "at least" or "no more than."

Even when the relationship itself is not linear, transformation into linear form is often easy. Relationships characterized by a constant percentage change—exponential relationships—become linear when expressed in logarithms. Total production cost, including both the fixed and variable components, is hyperbolic in form: $y = \frac{1}{x} + c$, in its simplest form. By substituting $z = \frac{1}{x}$, and maximizing z, we can minimize x. Such usable tricks are familiar to anyone with a moderate training in mathematics, or even just a little imagination. For a broad range of middle management decisions, data from repetitive operations are usually available for linear programming estimate of extremal points, by setting them up as a series of simultaneous equations which can be solved by the simplex method. The latter is not a particularly complicated process, being essentially the method learned by most of us in high school, except that in linear programming, we usually do not have enough equations to solve every variable and must use the computer for a tedious cut-and-try approach.

A highly simplified textbook problem illustrates the basic principle: [2]

The maker of both passenger cars and trucks has a factory divided into two shops: (1) The Assembly Shop 1, which requires 5 man-days for a truck and 2 man-days for each passenger vehicle; (2) Shop 2, which does the finishing at the rate of 3 man-days per vehicle, whether passenger car or truck. Shop 1 uses 180 man-days per week at capacity operation, Shop 2, 150 man-days per week. Profit on each truck completed is $300, on each passenger car $200. To maximize operating profit, what mix of trucks and passenger cars should be scheduled?

In mathematical notation, the problem is stated as follows:

If x_1 = no. of trucks made, x_2 = no. of cars, then we seek the values of x_1 and x_2 which satisfy the following conditions:
$$5x_1 + 2x_2 \leqq 180$$
$$\text{and} \quad 3x_1 + 3x_2 \leqq 150$$
Subject to the restrictions that:
$300x_1 + 200x_2$ has at least one real maximum value
and $x_1 \geqq 0 \leqq x_2$ (that is, that some cars and/or trucks will be built)

Every possible solution to the problem as thus defined lies in the shaded area of the graph in Figure 8-3, page 213. Not all of the infinity of points in this area are at the maximum, of course, and in this case, only one is. The maximum can only be found by comparing all that could be at the maximum. Fortunately, this includes only those points at one of the line intersections, as indicated.

Were there not some such limit on the number of solutions, even a computer would be useless; the number of possible points is truly infinite.

Not all such problems are soluble; sometimes the conditions are incompatible. Sometimes there are two or more solutions meeting all conditions equally, and management will make a choice between them on some other basis.

[2] Adapted from Kemeny, Schleifer, Snell, and Thompson, *Finite Mathematics with Business Applications* (Englewood Cliffs, N.J.: Prentice-Hall, Inc., 1962), pp. 379-380.

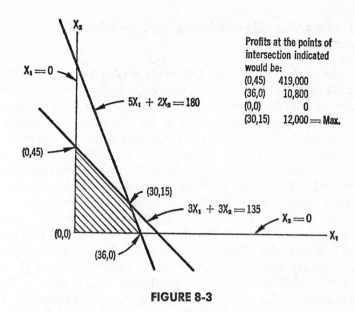

X_2

$X_1 = 0$

$5X_1 + 2X_2 = 180$

Profits at the points of
intersection indicated
would be:
(0,45)   419,000
(36,0)   10,800
(0,0)   0
(30,15)   12,000 = Max.

(0,45)

(30,15)

$3X_1 + 3X_2 = 135$

$X_2 = 0$

(0,0)

(36,0)

X_1

FIGURE 8-3

Linear programming finds increasingly wide utility at the operating level, where experience from past operations can form a reliable basis for estimating the future. In a form known as the *transportation model*, it has proven to be an excellent algorithm for determining warehouse locations.

But linear programming does not fit the need of every kind of allocation problem. The Young and Rubicam advertising agency, after thorough experimentation, came to the conclusion that recommendations for advertising media scheduling developed through linear programming were not optimum. Instead, they worked out a quite different kind of model dubbed the "High Assay Model," based on the rule of using the most productive medium up to the hilt, then the next most productive up to its margin, etc.[3] Linear programming does not give this kind of result.

[3] William T. Moran, "Practical Media Models Decisions and the Computer," *Journal of Marketing*, Vol. 27, No. 3 (July, 1963), pp. 26-30.

Finding Out Where Change Will Stabilize: The Markov Chain

Some mention has already been made in Chapter 2 of the utility of tables of transitional probabilities, otherwise known as *Markov chains* or *Markov processes,* when it was shown how information on what was happening during a period of flux could be used to tell what the underlying probability of the change was and where it would end, using as an example brand switching during a new product introduction. This example made use of a *nonabsorbing chain,* called thus because none of the transitions were irreversible. There was no brand of detergent so completely preferred, in our example, that none of the users, once they tried it, would not go back to some other brand. But there are various kinds of changes over time in business and elsewhere in which some of the states are *absorbing.* Once the change reaches one of these states, there is no reversal. Consider, for instance, the following table, showing the experience of a hypothetical trailer rental agency operating in three cities: A, B, and C. While the majority of the rentals are for local use, trailers are rented on a one-way basis and thus may start in any one of the three cities and end up in any other of the three. But trailers may come to another kind of end, too: They may be stolen or wrecked. Such trailers never return; they reach an *absorbing state,* as shown in the following table giving a typical month's experience:

TABLE 8-1. Starting Point and Destination of Drivuron Trailers Rented During the Month

(In percentages of those from the designated origin)

Place of Origin	Terminal City or Condition			
	A	B	C	Lost or Wrecked (L)
A	58	20	19	3
B	18	63	15	4
C	13	21	62	1
Lost, wrecked (L)	0	0	0	100

TABLE 8-1. (Cont.)

Computational Format

	L	A	B	C
L	1	0	0	0
A	.03	.58	.20	.19
B	.04	.18	.63	.15
C	.01	.13	.21	.62

If we change the percentages to decimals, we have a table of transition probabilities, or a Markov matrix, with one absorbing state, *lost or wrecked.* If no new trailers are purchased, we need no computer to calculate the end result: all trailers will finally end up lost or wrecked. If we had more than one absorbing state —if, for example, trailers were sold on reaching a certain point of service or dilapidation—we would have to make a calculation to determine how many would end up in each of the absorbing states.

But our principal interest is likely to be in the answers to some different questions:

1. How long, on the average, will it be before the process is absorbed? In terms of our illustration, how long will a trailer be in service, on the average?
2. How many periods of time will the process be in each non-absorbing state? That is, how many months is a trailer likely to be in each of the cities during its term of service?
3. How much input is needed to stabilize the process at some desired point of equilibrium. How many trailers must we buy each month to hold the stock at the current level?
4. At what points in the process should the input be injected to hold the process in some form of desired balance? In this case, where should we have new trailers shipped to start their service, A, B, or C, and in what proportion? If we look at the original table, we can see that A loses more to B and C than it gets back from either. Likewise, C ships more to B than it gets in return.

The answers to each of these questions comes from a different calculation, but one that follows a generalized standard and is a simple computer program. Even for a highly simplified illustration such as the one given, the tedium of calculation requires a computer, and even a short explanation of the process requires use of matrix notation. Those who are familiar with this form of mathematical symbolism, will find an explanation of nonabsorbing chains and some uses in Kemeny, et al., *Finite Mathematics with Business Applications* (Prentice-Hall, Inc., 1962), pages 282-298.

In other types of problems, other questions would be asked, and a calculable answer would be available. For example, one whole branch of Markov analysis deals with waiting line, or *Queueing* problems. The line at the supermarket can fluctuate erratically in length. The states of nature of interest to the store management would be the various possible lengths of line, and the units of time measurement would be the smallest interval of time in which at least one customer would arrive at the counter. Presumably, management's interest would lie in balancing out two antithetical costs: (1) the costs of checkout clerks, whose number determines the maximum length a line can attain, and (2) loss of good will and patronage from impatient customers. With some empirical observation on line lengths and customer time intervals and service intervals, he can find out how long the line will grow with any counter checkout force. His estimate of the cost of this force is likely to be very accurate, but he will have more difficulty determining the costs and probabilities of patronage loss due to waiting, i.e., just how long, on the average, and at the maximum, a line can get before significant numbers of customers shift at least part of their buying elsewhere, and how much loss this will entail. But there is such a cost, and if he can make a rough estimate, he will know how many counters he should operate and with what personnel.

While the details of the calculations are not particularly intricate, mastering the tedious procedure requires hours of drill and had best be done in a mathematics course. The computer programming needed is standard, and very simple. The important thing, as with all these mathematical implements, is to understand its uses and meaning. Outside of production processes, it is safe to say most of the uses of Markov chains have not even been explored. One interested mathematician has used it to analyze a department store's charge account system, determining what the distribution of delinquency can be expected to approach after a period of time, and in what length of time. (The absorbing states were two here: bad debts turned over for collection and paid-up customers.) He has also experimented with it to project the expected teaching load in a graduate program subject to student turnover due to transfers and other causes and thus to estimate the intake permissible with a given available teaching staff. By analogy, a firm with a large management training program could estimate the needed recruit intake to get the eventual supply of middle and top managers needed. Although no case has come to public attention, Markov analysis of a mail-order customer file would seem a useful way of predicting how long a customer will remain active.

As with most mathematical calculations, the actual answers that come out of a Markov analysis look very precise. But their true accuracy is no greater than the accuracy of the somewhat limited empirical observations on which the initial probablity tables are built. The approximations resulting are, of course, far better than we are likely to use in the absence of such analyses and are normally quite adequate to the needs of business decision.

Summary

1. The aim of some strategic and most operating choices is to achieve some optimum point in the cost-volume-profit relationship. Four useful special tools have come out of modern mathematics to help us in determining what is optimum: (1) sequential decision theory to help determine the best decision path when the value of any choice depends on the outcome of later choices which will have to follow, (2) Gantt Charts and network analysis to determine the best timing of complex tasks, (3) the extremal methods of calculus and linear programming to determine optimum values of known interrelationships, and (4) Markov analysis

to assist in finding out what the end results of a transition situation are likely to be.

2. Some of the alternatives faced in many decision situations simply eventuate in a need to make further decisions, sometimes in a chain of decision-event-decision-event, etc. Statistical decision theory offers a method of working back from what is known about the end result and each preceding step to get an *expected value* for each decision, and also the value of any added information needed.

3. The timing of operation sequences is an important element of cost attacked first in terms of the simple graphic device of the Gantt Chart, and now, in the two main variations of network analysis: Critical Path Method (CPM) and Program Evaluation and Review Technique (PERT). The aim of both methods is to identify the critical task sequences and the necessary starting times of these few components of a complex task which can influence the attainment of the completion target date.

4. The optimum combination of factors or other inputs usually requires some kind of calculation. Calculus has long been the mainstay of determination of maxima and minima of physical measurements. But the precision of measurement required and knowledge of relationships are too great for most business problems. In addition, calculus is of value only when relationships are curvilinear, whereas most of the data we deal with in business seems to approximate straight line relationships or is transformable into straight line form. The technique of linear programming makes use of computer iteration to try the various possible solutions to find any maxima or minima that may exist in the inter-relationships.

5. Markov chain analysis uses data on the changes taking place as estimates of transition probabilities, and analyzes these to estimate where the change is leading. A form of particular interest is so-called absorbing chain analysis, in which one or more of the transitions is irreversible, permitting us to estimate what inputs may be needed to keep the process moving at some desired level, the length of time an item may move through the process before reaching the irreversible state, and the costs of changing some of the values.

Selected Bibliography

I. REALISTIC DISCUSSION OF THE NATURE OF COMPETITION

Bain, Joe S., *Barriers to New Competition*. Cambridge, Mass.: Harvard University Press, 1956. The practical factors limiting the number of competitors.

Chamberlin, Edward H., *The Theory of Monopolistic Competition* (8th ed.), Cambridge, Mass.: Harvard University Press, 1962. The first half of this edition is the historic published version of the author's doctoral dissertation, but the last half adds a number of appendices covering the history of the early development of monopolistic competition theory, a definition of selling costs, and other later reflections which are important. His careful distinction between his concept of product differentiation and Joan Robinson's quite different concept of imperfect competition needs a wider reading among economists.

————, *Towards a More General Theory of Value*. Oxford: The Oxford University Press, 1957. A collection of essays delineating the author's mature reflections and expansions on the implications of the concept of monopolistic competition.

Clark, J. M., *Competition as a Dynamic Process*. Washington, D.C.: The Brookings Institution, 1961. A successful attempt to explore thoroughly the implications of the concepts of product differentiation and innovation for the dynamics of competition, both from the standpoint of managerial policy and that of economic welfare.

II. MANAGEMENT OF PRODUCT AND INNOVATION [1]

Berg, Thomas L. and Schuchman, Abe (eds.), *Product Strategy and Management*. New York: Holt, Rinehart & Winston, Inc., 1963. A

---

[1] The brevity of this list reflects the lack of attention which has been bestowed on this aspect of economics.

collection of periodical articles attempting to cover every aspect of product management.

Drucker, Peter F., *Managing for Results*. New York: Harper & Row, Publishers, Inc., 1964. Deals at length, among other aspects of management, with an original and interesting framework for analysis of product policy and product strategy.

III. PRICING AS PRACTICED

Haynes, W. W., *Pricing Decisions in a Small Business*. Lexington, Ky.: University of Kentucky, 1962. Analysis of a study of actual pricing practices of sample small firms.

Holdren, Bob R., *The Structure of a Retail Market and the Market Behavior of Retail Units*. Englewood Cliffs, N.J.: Prentice-Hall, Inc., 1960. A study of the pricing practices of a number of supermarket chains, with special attention to the strategy of the price-mix and loss-leaders.

Kaplan, A. D. H., Dirlam, Joel B., and Lanzillotti, Robert F., *Pricing in Big Business*. Washington, D.C.: The Brookings Institution, 1958. Case studies of the price practices of twenty of the largest corporations.

Oxenfeldt, Alfred R., *Pricing for Marketing Executives*. San Francisco: Wadsworth Publishing Company, 1961 (paperback). A compact attempt to integrate recognition of the institutional arrangements and business practice considerations in pricing with the insights and concepts developed by economists.

————, "Multi-Stage Approach to Pricing," *Harvard Business Review*, July-August, 1960. A proposed approach to pricing decision which narrows down the alternatives to be considered through a systematic elimination of choices which do not accord with the firm's marketing niche, resources, and marketing plans.

IV. ECONOMIC COST

Clark, J. M., *Studies in the Economics of Overhead Costs*. Chicago: University of Chicago Press, 1923. The classical definitive study of economic cost measurement.

Dean, Joel, "Cost Structures of Enterprises and Break-even Techniques," *American Economic Review* (May, 1948). The essence of this article is also in Joel Dean, *Managerial Economics,* Englewood Cliffs, N.J.: Prentice-Hall, Inc., 1951, pages 326-341.

Johnston, J., *Statistical Cost Analysis.* New York: McGraw-Hill Book Co., Inc., 1960. A critical review and analysis of a number of empirical studies of actual cost structures.

Keller, I. Wayne, *Management Accounting for Profit Control.* New York: McGraw-Hill Book Co., Inc., 1957. One of a large number of accounting textbooks with a reasonably adequate discussion of costing from the accountant's standpoint.

V. CAPITAL BUDGETING

Bierman, Harold, Jr. and Smidt, Seymour, *The Capital Budgeting Decision.* New York: The Macmillan Company, 1961. A thorough but reasonably concise discussion of the economics of capital budgeting.

Gordon, Myron J., *The Investment, Financing, and Valuation of the Corporation.* Homewood, Ill.: Richard D. Irwin, Inc., 1962. Includes discussion of the problems involved when trying to evaluate alternatives with varying degrees of associated risk.

Lindsay, Robert and Sametz, Arnold W., *Financial Management: An Analytical Approach.* Homewood, Ill.: Richard D. Irwin, Inc., 1963. Contains a thorough and easily followed discussion of the pros and cons of the major procedures for evaluating capital investment.

Solomon, Ezra (ed.), *The Management of Corporate Capital.* Chicago: The University of Chicago Press, 1959. A collection of papers on various aspects of capital budgeting.

Terbourgh, George, *Business Investment Policy.* Washington, D.C.: Machinery and Allied Products Institute, 1958. Outlines and discusses the MAPI formula for calculating investment return, applicable mainly to evaluation of replacement.

VI. MATHEMATICAL TOOLS FOR ECONOMIC ANALYSIS [2]

Dorfman, Robert, Samuelson, Paul A., and Solow, Robert M., *Linear Programming and Economic Analysis.* New York: McGraw-Hill Book Co., Inc., 1958. A thorough and largely non-mathematical dis-

---

[2] None of the following require more than an initial familiarity with ordinary algebra.

cussion of the related techniques of linear programming and game theory, the possible applications of linear algebra to economic analysis, and the limitations of game theory in relation to business decision. A brief exposition of matrix algebra is included in the appendix for those wishing for a concise run-through of this form of notation.

Kemeny, John G., Schleifer, Arthur, Jr., Snell, J. Laurie, and Thompson, Gerald L., *Finite Mathematics with Business Applications*. Englewood Cliffs, N.J.: Prentice-Hall, Inc., 1962. A text giving complete elementary coverage to mathematical logic, statistical decision theory, matrix algebra, linear programming, and game theory. Assumes an elementary knowledge of ordinary algebra.

Manne, Alan S., *Economic Analysis for Business Decisions*. New York: McGraw-Hill Book Co., Inc., 1961. For those with a limited mathemathical background, another concise discussion of linear programming (including the transportation model), integer programming, and decision trees.

Schlaifer, Robert, *Introduction to Statistics for Business Decisions*. New York: McGraw-Hill Book Co., Inc., 1961. The standard text on the use of the Bayesian approach to statistical decision.

Index

Algebra, matrix, 45
Algorithm, critical path, 198-201
Analysis, business, concepts needed for, 1
  frequency curve, 35-40
  normal curve, 36-38
  trend, 40-44
Averages, 25

Benefit, perception of, 80-81
  product, 80
Breadwinners, today's, 107
  tomorrow's, 107
  yesterday's, 108
Break-even, as form of analytical simulation, 49-52

Calculus, differential, 210-211
Capital, standpipe, 179
  start-up, 177-178
  working, 177-178
Capital budgeting, 163-180
  learning from mistakes in, 175
  for new products, 168
  precision of, 164
Certainties, near, 15
Chamberlain, Edward H., 2, 78
Change, revealing forces underlying, 45
Cinderellas, 108
Clark, J. M., 62, 78, 84, 115
Competition, aim of, 3
  chain, 84
  definition of, 6
  effective, 84-87
  four variables of, 78

Competition (*Cont.*)
  models of, 83-87
  monopolistic, 2, 84-87
    graphic analogy, 85-86
  product line, 105-107
Cost, accountability and, 148
  contribution to fixed, 49, 50
  controllable, 148
  definition of, 7
  direct, 154
  discretionary, 51
  economic, 147-162
  escapable, 151
  incremental, 149
  imputed, 148-149
  indirect, 154
  inescapable, 160
  joint, 155-159
  of not-doing, 148
  opportunity, 149-151
  outlay, 149-151
  past, as basis for estimating future, 148
  postponable, 152
  programmed, 51, 160
  selling, as production, 81-82
  stairstep, 159-160
  standard, 154-155
  standby, 151
  sunk, 152-153
  unavoidable, 151
  urgent, 152
Counting, double, 25
Critical Path Method (CPM), 191-210

Demand, behavior of, 66-71
  measurement of relationships, 61-66

Demand (*Cont.*)
  nature of, 55-61
    consumer example, 56-58
    industrial example, 58-59
Demand and supply, forecasting, 55-76
Depreciation, 25, 153-154
  obsolescence, 153
  wear-and-tear, 153
Desire, customer changeability, 89
Differentiation, ephemeral nature of, 90
  inescapability of, 87-88
  psychological basis for, 82
Discount, example, 28-32
  uncertainty, 27-34
  time, 11
Discount structure, as a buying price, 128
Discounting, present value, 171-173
  rate of return, 171-173
Drucker, Peter F., 95, 107

Economic concepts basic to decision, 1-21
Economic cost, versus accounting cost, 9
Economics, price, traditional static, 83-84
Elasticity of demand, cross-section analysis of, 64-65
  margin, 62-63
  nature of, 59-60
  price, 63
  quantification of experience as estimate basis, 65-66
  time series analysis of, 64
Equimarginalism, 10
Expenditures, discretionary, 152
Experience, as a set of probabilities, 35-36

Failures, obvious, 108
Fair trade, 139-141
Figures, need for using, 22-23
  understanding the meaning of, 23-27
Forecasting, the art of, 12-17
  conceptual basis for, 1

Forecasting (*Cont.*)
  cost reduction, 167-168
  of investment outlays and income, 166-168
Forces, hidden, analysis for, 34-38
Frequency distributions, comparison of, 39-40

Gantt Chart, 191
Goods, capital, 70
  consumer, high-order differentiation, 67-68
  low-order differentiation, 67
  consumer durable, 69-70
  homogeneous, 67

Heuristic rules, 164
Hunch, 13
Hypothesis, 13

Income, price-volume, 52
Incrementalism, 9
Industry, problem of defining, 84
Innovation, in accompanying services, 92
  by advertising insights, 3
  as basis for success, 3
  as dependability of supply, 93
  difficulty of predicting, 3
  evolutionary, 104
  forms of, 91-93
  as idea, 91
  matching firm's area of excellence, 102-103
  psychological, 89
  research role in, 90-91
  resource requirements for, 103-105
  revolutionary, 104-105
  sources of potential, 93-101
  by uniformity of quality, 92
Integration, vertical, 88
Investment, choice of best alternative, 174-175
  consideration of economic life, 174
  definition, 8
  discounting for uncertainty, 174

Investment (*Cont.*)
discounting value of for time, 169-174
making sure of alternatives, 164-166
in management ego, 108
timing of, 176-177

Joint products, types of, 156

Kemeny, John G., et al., 212-213, 216

Law, 13
Levy, Ferdinand K., 191-210
Linear programming, 211-213

Margin elasticity, 62-63
Marginalism, 9
Market segment, 79
Markov chains, absorbing, 45, 214-217
nonabsorbing, 45-48
Markov processes, *see* Markov chains
Materials, raw, 71
Matrix, transitional probability, 46
Model, definition, 13
Money, cost of, 175-176
Monopoly, mountain peak, 85
valley, 85

Nature, state of, 45, 47
Network analysis, 191-210

Oligopolies, chain, 84
price behavior of, 71
Opportunity, alternate, as basic yardstick, 8-12
Optimum points, methods for pinpointing, 210-213
Overhead, contribution to, 159

Pay-back period, 169-170
Pay-out period, 52
Patterns, brand switching, 46-48
seasonal, 16

Percentages, 25
PERT, 191
Perspective, time, 12
Point, fixed, 45, 47
Predictability, evaluating, 15
Price, administered, 113
buyer's key role in, 113
consumer credit, 143-144
control of, 142-143
cost standard for, 133
definition, 7
distributive discount structure, 128-130
decisions on structure, 126-130
fair, standards, 132-133
as incentive, 141-142
latitude for decision on, 113
leadership, 138-139
maintenance of, 139-141
off-season and special group, 137-138
product line structure, 126-128
psychological aspects of, 130-133
quantum effects, 131
reverse direction perception, 132
as a tactical weapon, 112-146
temporary reduction of, 134-135
types of decision on, 112
Pricing, differentiated, bid prices, 121-126
complex standard products, 120-121
dynamic and tactical aspects of, 133-141
engineering to a price, 115-117
incremental, 136-137
new products, 136
promotional, 135-136
situations, types of, 127
stripped models, 127
target, 117-120
break-even, 119
cost-plus-a-profit, 117-118
return-on-investment, 118
uniform industry, competitive, 115-116
traditional, 114
Probability, subjective, 17, 32-34
transitional, 45, 214

Product, categories of elements, 107-108
    classification of packages, 66-71
    compatibility with producer's abilities, 102-105
    definition, 2
    development of, 108
    for the future that is here, 94-96
    management of, 77-111
    physical form, 78-80
    planning, 88-89
    as principal variable, 77-78
    that is not a product, 108
    as value, 78
Production defined, 6
Profit, forecasting maximum, 17

Queueing, 216

Rates, 25
Repair jobs, 108
Resource allocation to product line, 107-109
Risk, affordability, 188
    calculable, 16
Rules of thumb, 164

Schleifer, Arthur, Jr., *see* Kemeny, et al.
Segmentation of market, definition, 2
Sequential decision, meaning of results, 189-190
    method of evaluating, 182-190
    source of data, 188-189

Services, construction, 70
    preference creating, 59
Simulation, 49-53
Sleepers, 108
Snell, J. Laurie, *see* Kemeny et al.
Specialties, productive, 107-108
    unjustified, 108
    unnecessary, 108
State, absorbing, 215
Strategy, competitive bidding, 123-126
Substitutability, 82
Supplies, industrial, 71
Supply, management of, 73-74

Terbourgh, George, 173-174
Theory, 13
Thompson, Gerald L., 191-210, 212-213
Timing of task components, 190-210
Tools, mathematical, 22-54, 123-126, 181-218
Trends, analysis of, 26-27
    need to learn "why," 41-42

Uncertainties, estimable, 16
Unknowables, 17
Utility of return, 188

Value, discounted expected, 18
Value concepts, basic economic, 4

Wiest, Jerome D., 191-210